With very best wishes

John le Carré

27th April 1985

Nosework for Dogs

Nosework for Dogs

Tracking and Related Applications

John Cree

PELHAM BOOKS · LONDON

First published in Great Britain by
Pelham Books Ltd
44 Bedford Square
London WC1B 3DU
1980

ISBN 0 7207 1212 2

Typeset by Cambrian Typesetters, Farnborough, Hants
Printed and bound in Great Britain by
Billing & Sons Limited, Guildford, London and Worcester

To MY FATHER,
whose example in life has greatly
influenced my consideration
towards our canine companions

Contents

Acknowledgments

As this is a publication about dogs and their scenting ability, I must give pride of place to the dogs themselves. Without Quest, my first German Shepherd, who introduced me to this fascinating subject I would not have started to collect the knowledge which has gone into this book. The female members of our canine family have all given me a more exacting job in channelling their scenting activities and through them I have learnt much more about the canine mind and its application to scenting.

Beginners who have let me help them at the start of their careers or those who have sought out my assistance when in difficulty have all helped by creating a challenge which inevitably resulted in an increase of knowledge through success or failure. The opportunities to steward, tracklay and judge at competitive events have all created another breeding ground for thought, theories and conclusions. All of these situations have played their part in this quest for knowledge.

Irene, my wife, has played a big part in vetting and typing the manuscript. My thanks also go to Fiona McFadyen and my son-in-law, Colin Ball, for helping to ensure that the manuscript was technically presentable. Doris Allan was wholly responsible for the sketches; I could only give her a rough outline of my requirements but her ingenuity, artistic ability and knowledge of the subject is there for all to see.

Abbreviations

C.D.	Companion Dog
Ch.	Champion
Ex.	Excellent
G.S.D.	German Shepherd Dog
Int.	International
Ob.	Obedience
P.D.	Police Dog
T.D.	Tracker Dog
U.D.	Utility Dog
W.D.	Working Dog
W.T.	Working Trials
X.	Excellent

Introduction

Every dog loves to use his nose. He can be seen following the scent of a rabbit or some other game whilst his owner takes him for a walk through the countryside. He can also enjoy struggling through undergrowth to seek out a stick which has been thrown by his master or searching a pebbled beach for a thrown stone and confounding everybody by bringing back the correct one. There can also be great fun hunting with the children during a game of hide and seek; one child may hide from the others and defy all efforts to highlight the hiding place but include the family pet to aid the seeking party and success can be guaranteed in record time. These are the joys of the family dog, joys which have now been harnessed and controlled by man to aid police forces, the services, mountain rescue operations and in the competitive field of working trials and obedience competitions. Trained dogs can track down a fugitive, quarter an area in search of a criminal or missing person, can be used for the location of drugs, explosives or buried bodies. Searching through the undergrowth for lost property or discriminating and acknowledging articles with a selected individual's scent are additional functions for our canine friends.

Any dog's greatest asset is his inherited power of scenting, even the Gazehounds who depend on quickness of the eye and are not generally considered to be noseworkers have a sense of smell far greater than that of man. We cannot compete against our canine companions; even in this day of high technology there is not a piece of equipment which can replace a dog's ability to follow the track from a human being or differentiate between the scent from one person and another.

This book has been written primarily for those wishing to make practical use of their dog's inherited scenting instinct, either in a professional capacity or for the owner with a competitive spirit who wishes to train for working trials or obedience competitions. The training principles should also prove to be of value and interest to the family dog owner who is looking for greater companionshop through a fuller development of his dog's character.

The contents are also based on the applications involving human scent only, with a full understanding of tracking as a basis for all other scenting applications.

Training in this field of work is not necessarily restricted to particular working breeds and it is remarkable what some of the more unlikely breeds are capable of achieving. It is natural that the recognized noseworking breeds have an advantage, but that should not stop the owner of a less likely breed, crossbreed or even mongrel from developing his dog's inheritance to the full.

Many family dog owners become very competitive minded and make dog training their hobby. Working trials and obedience competitions provide an outlet where tracking and other scenting tests are included in a fuller schedule of work. Other owners are perfectly happy to apply some informal training where they can show their family and friends that the house pet is more than just a lovable character.

A dog's sense of smell must have taken many centuries to develop, let us help him enjoy and pass on his inheritance to future generations.

1

Your Dog's Inheritance

Before domestication a dog's nose was a major part of his survival kit; the use of his nose, ears and eyes was developed in varying degrees to cater for local requirements. He had to eat to live and to eat generally meant locating and catching each meal.

Although the senses which controlled his hearing were mainly developed as part of the defence warning system, they also served to let him know that a meal ticket might well be in the vicinity. Eyesight became an important factor where the countryside afforded little or no cover and the visual movement of game was the first indication of a prospective meal. Keen eyesight could pick out movement at a distance and survival would be dependent on the ability to detect these distant movements. Dogs in this category were the forerunners of our present group of breeds known as Gazehounds.

With most types of dog, however, his sense of smell was the main tool in his kit for survival. When an animal was close enough on the windward side of the dog, the animal could easily be located and considered as suitable prey. Experience told him if the particular scent warranted investigation or if the animal was healthy and belonged to a stronger family.

Tracking down an animal, be it weak, injured or a type easily overcome, was the main approach to securing food for most dogs. The scent such an animal left on the ground, the scent of crushed vegetation or disturbed soil from its foot or hoof prints, was followed by these dogs until they could catch up with their prey. To locate the ground scent of an animal and to track in the wrong direction would end in frustration and hunger. Sensitivity was, therefore, developed through the survival of the keenest noseworkers who knew when a faint track was present and were able to detect the correct direction. Centuries of survival of these highly developed scenting instincts have created the forerunners of our present-day tracking breeds.

Since dogs became more attached to man, domestication has created a situation where survival has been less dependent on the dog's own abilities. However, the instincts built up over many centuries do not disappear very easily.

For many years now breeding has been taken out of the hands of mother nature and man's manipulation of matings has secured the strengths of inherited instincts to suit his own requirements. Man has developed dogs that hunt by sight or by scent and the fast sprinters who require keen eyesight with a quick burst of speed to catch their prey. These were the forerunners to our present Greyhounds and such like. Then there were the scenting hunters who could flush out game for their human companions to spear or shoot according to the times; these were the predecessors to our present-day Gundogs. The development of terriers as vermin hunters proved to be effective with aggressive little dogs round the villages and farms keeping the rodents at bay. Then there were the shepherding dogs which have resulted in a variety of breeds capable of carrying out many functions for present-day society.

Although every dog has scenting abilities far superior to that of man, the development of certain species has resulted in breeds, or families of breeds, which are recognized as specialists in this field. There is no doubt that, of the more common breeds, the best noseworkers come from the gundog or shepherding families, with a greater likelihood of a strong scenting instinct from the progeny of generations of working stock.

Unfortunately, over the years the introduction of breed exhibiting has brought a new dimension to the various breed characteristics and, although this has certainly helped to standardize and improve the construction within each breed, the working qualities seem to have been ignored by many breeders. Some breeds would appear to have resulted in two distinct types where one is the result of selective breeding to achieve a more fashionable show specimen. As many breeders lack practical knowledge of the working requirements of their dogs they are not in a position to give proper consideration to perpetuating the inherited instincts which have made their breed so special in that particular field of work. On the other hand the working specimens of a particular breed tend to be selected from very keen natural workers who are suitably constructed for the job in hand. The continual breeding from these lines will certainly help to maintain the natural gifts inherited by that particular species.

This does not mean that dogs bred for the show ring are unsuited for work but it does mean that a much higher proportion may have an ever diminishing natural aptitude for nosework.

One may think that because a person has chosen a dog of a particular breed that the animal will have a natural talent for his selected type of work, but the variation within any species can be quite extensive. The Border Collie has been bred through many generations as a sheep or cattle worker, but a shepherd will select the best of a litter and will discard any puppies which do not appear to have sufficient natural instinct to simplify the task of training. A shepherd will not waste time and effort without a reasonable guarantee of a suitable return. The police will view a number of German Shepherd Dogs before selecting suitable material for the varying tasks which require good, stable, all-round workers. A gamekeeper will dispose of unlikely stock so that maximum return can be gained from his most natural and promising youngsters.

Puppies who finish up as family pets, whether they come from show stock or working lines, or are simply crossbreeds may well prove to have exceptionally strong scenting instincts or may, by canine standards, have little interest in using their ever-diminishing natural instincts.

Each dog owner can, however, capitalize on what natural ability his dog does possess. This natural instinct may not be particularly evident but the correct inducements may well reveal those hidden talents.

2

Outlets for Scenting Activity

The outlets for scenting activities are as numerous as they are varied; these activities themselves may require a brief introduction and can be placed into the following categories:

Tracking To follow the scent left on the ground by a person walking over that ground. To track down a criminal, to find a missing person, or to locate articles dropped en route.

Seek Back To track back and find an article dropped or lost by the dog owner whilst out for a walk.

Property Search To find articles which have been lost by a person in either light or heavy undergrowth.

Quartering Air or wind scenting to quarter over open ground, through thickets or buildings, to locate criminals or missing persons.

Scent Discrimination This is basically an application for obedience competitions where the dog is required to pick out an article amongst many others after being given the scent from the individual who initially scented the wanted article.

The outlets for these applications can also be put into the following general categories: professional, competitive or household pleasure.

THE PROFESSIONAL DOG
This category will include the police, the armed forces, security work and mountain rescue work.

Some dogs may be trained for a single specialized purpose such as that of drug detection, or possibly to indicate the presence of explosives. There are many other specialized applications but all are based on air scenting for hidden goods or ground scenting for items buried under the ground.

Other dogs are trained to wind or air scent to locate a hidden intruder, criminal or missing person. This could take place out in the open where there are fields and hedgerows or woods with thick undergrowth. An enclosed factory yard may require to be searched where machinery scattered around can afford many hiding places. Warehouses and large shops can be the subject of an intensive search for a reported intruder and it is remarkable the hiding places these villains can find but a well-educated dog will always locate and indicate the presence of the offending party.

Both the wind and ground scenting applications have been extended to mountain rescue work where dogs can pick up the scent of an injured person who could easily be obscured from view by rocks or undergrowth or, alternatively, when people are buried beneath the snow resulting from an avalanche.

Security duties for the armed forces or commercial security organizations enable our canine friends to use their acute sense of hearing or smell as required to indicate the presence of an intruder where a natural or acquired sense of protection will ensure a suitable warning. Tracking is a very important activity for a working police dog, with the armed forces now realizing the full advantage of a good, sound, tracking dog under terrorist conditions.

THE COMPETITIVE DOG
Civilian obedience tests or working trials give a tremendous amount of scope for the family pet. Nearly four hundred obedience shows are held each year throughout the UK and approximately forty working trials will span the same period.

About six hundred Kennel Club registered training clubs

are spread throughout the country and cater for competitive and domestic obedience training. Training societies for working trials are not so numerous and may only amount to about twenty in all. The Kennel Club Regulations governing the requirements for both Working Trials (S.1) and Obedience (S.2) are given in the appendices but a brief resumé of the requirements for competition will help the reader to understand the terminology used throughout this book.

Obedience shows can be held within a large hall or outdoors in a park, depending on the time of year and weather conditions. These shows are normally a one-day affair with Saturday being the most popular.

By a series of wins a dog can progress through each stage (Class) as follows:

1. Pre-Beginners
2. Beginners
3. Novice
4. Class 'A'
5. Class 'B'
6. Class 'C'

The tests involve precision control and a build-up through each stage with variations of heel work, recalls, retrieving, distance control, send away, stays and scent discrimination.

Most shows are designated as Open with some forty or so each year carrying a Championship title. Winning a Championship Class 'C' gains a dog an Obedience Certificate and three such certificates under different judges make a dog into an Obedience Champion.

Working trials are outdoor events and are usually held regardless of the weather. These events normally last from two to five days depending on the size of entry although each dog will only be required to attend on one or two of these days. The amount of ground required to hold these events will usually be equivalent in size to two top-class golf courses.

Dogs progress through each stage (Stake) by a series of qualifications and the progression is as follows:

1.   C.D. (Companion Dog)   an optional Stake
2.   U.D. (Utility Dog)   a qualifying Stake

3.	W.D. (Working Dog)	a qualifying Stake
4.(a)	T.D. (Tracker Dog)	open stake
4.(b)	P.D. (Police Dog)	open stake and equal in status to T.D.

Dogs must qualify through U.D., W.D., and T.D. at Open Trials to enter equivalent stakes at Championship Trials and thereby gain the appropriate titles. A similar progression is required to compete for the P.D. title, although qualification in P.D. at Open Trials is not necessary. Most civilian handlers aim for the T.D. Stake although a few do train their dogs for both T.D. and P.D.

Winning Open Stakes either T.D. or P.D. at Championship Trials gains a dog a Working Trials Certificate. Two such certificates gained under different judges will make a dog into a Working Trials Champion.

The working trials tests involve control work, which may be considered similar to the obedience tests although less precision is required. There are agility tests which regulate the size and type of dog progressing to the top stake and there is nosework which includes tracking and property searching. The P.D. Stake also includes criminal work (patrol) which involves wind scenting for the location of a missing person or criminal.

The American regulations differ considerably from those in the UK. The United States obedience trials utilize one scent discrimination test with two different kinds of article. The tracking test stands on its own for the coveted tracking title.

It is not the intention of this book to go into the full training requirements for every exercise in UK obedience shows, working trials or US obedience trials. The contents have, however, been prepared to give a specialized 'in depth' approach to the training and competitive requirements for the various scenting applications covered in the UK and US regulations.

The training for the scenting applications is usually treated as part of the normal obedience training but it does in fact require a different outlook and a greater understanding of a dog's natural ability to carry out a function we cannot possibly experience ourselves.

FOR HOUSEHOLD PLEASURE
Everybody likes a dog who shows his intelligence and every dog has something to offer his family, something he is proud of doing.

Your dog may like to find Dad's slippers when he comes home from work in the evening. This can be a game where sight may play a big part but he will still find them as easily in a darkened room where his scenting ability has to take over.

Finding the children at bed-time may require the sense of hearing for a general location, but these children know that if they hide and watch there is great fun in observing their pet darting here and there until he catches 'wind' of them.

A dog who is encouraged or taught to 'seek back' along the route you have just walked will return with a dropped glove or the car keys. One who has been taught to search can be invaluable when some important item has been lost in a picnic area.

There was one occasion when I had lost my new Parker pen. I did not even know if it was in my jacket pocket when we took the children out for a walk with Tanya, our new German Shepherd puppy and Quest, my working trials Shepherd. But there was one area of heavy grass where we had been playing with the dogs and the pen might have been knocked out of my jacket at that time.

It was some two hours later when Quest and I went back to that area of some fifty yards square to try and search for the missing pen. Quest worked away for some fifteen minutes or so when his head went right down into the heavy grass and he returned to me with his find. I could see no sign of a pen in his mouth and was disappointed when he dropped an ear clip into my hand. We went home realizing that this new pen, a gift, was lost and was unlikely to have been lost in that particular area which Quest had just searched.

I let Irene, my wife, see our find. She immediately put her hand to her ear and said 'Where did you find it?' I did not realize it was her ear clip and she had never missed it. Quest had done a good job.

Scent discrimination is a fine party trick where a playing card with the owner's scent can be picked out by the family pet when the full pack of cards has been scattered over the floor. There are many variations to this game.

As a golfer with a maximum handicap I found that Quest would help to minimize the cost of my deficiencies with the ease in which he could find my golf ball. His tracking background would help locate the resting place of my ball in the rough by tracking it from an early bounce.

One action of his which mystified my companions and two other golfers took place one evening when we were playing the seventeenth hole on the Monifieth Medal course. My left-handed slice from the tee headed for the semi-rough between the seventeenth and second fairways. As it was late in the evening two other golfers were practising on the second fairway; my ball had landed in the vicinity of some half-a-dozen practice balls. On arriving at the scene I was asked what kind of ball I was playing. I replied, 'A Bromford'. One golfer said, 'That's it over there, a Bromford black spot.' I replied that mine was a blue spot and was promptly told that I was mistaken. I looked at Quest and asked him to find it. He went round each ball sniffing before moving on to the next. He did not recognize any of the golf balls as mine. There was some heavy grass some ten yards away, an unkept bunker. I directed Quest over to the area. He sniffed around then stopped to indicate his find – he knew he was not allowed to pick up golf balls. There was my Bromford blue spot and two golfers completely mystified as to how Quest could tell the difference between one ball and another.

Dogs love to use their inherited scenting instinct. They seem to know how superior they are to man in this respect and are happy to carry out a unique service.

3

Choice of Dog

The choice of dog depends to a great extent on the owner's personal fancy and the reasons he has for keeping a dog in the first place.

Many people are loyal to one particular breed and it is not my intention to try and sway that loyalty towards any individual breed because I may consider it to have particular advantages. Loyalty to one's own breed can achieve greater satisfaction in overcoming problems and disadvantages than changing over to a more fashionable working breed for the sake of success. However, there are people with no particular loyalties who wish to consider various breeds before making a purchase and there are existing owners who may wish to understand the effort required to realize a dog's full potential or his possible limitations.

There is no doubt that the most popular breeds for scenting work come from the shepherding or gundog families. Although certain other species can show greater sensitivity in their scenting powers they may prove to require a much greater understanding, but success can certainly be very sweet to the owners of these working canine companions.

Of the shepherding family, the German Shepherd Dog (Alsatian) is the dog most universally used for scenting work. This breed can perform so many tasks, both scenting and physically, and he is such a natural all-rounder he must be considered to be the world's most versatile canine partner.

Although the Border Collie does not have the stature of the German Shepherd he has become a very strong favourite with obedience and working trials enthusiasts. His keenness to work and ability to make full use of nature's gift has put him right to the fore as a scent working dog.

Other less well-known shepherding breeds, such as the Groenendael, are evident in the working trials scene and have proved to be very effective.

The gundog family, however, supplies the greatest choice of different noseworking breeds. Hunters, past and present, have established a number of different breeds for varying purposes in their pursuit of game. There are dogs which point through their ability to wind scent, others which are bred to raise or retrieve game by wind scenting, and yet others which will track an injured bird or animal. There is no doubt that hunters of the past and gamekeepers of the present have done a tremendous amount to establish a family of breeds with exceedingly strong scenting instincts.

As a scent worker for non-hunting activities the Labrador Retriever must take pride of place. The police use many for drug detection and the army have also found them to be a most useful dog for property searching, where arms, ammunitions and explosives belonging to terrorists have to be located. They also seem to be the favourite as tracking dogs with many a terrorist finding that his invisible trail from the scene of an incident resulted in his capture. The Labrador is also very popular in the competitive field of working trials.

Sir Joseph Simpson, with Frenchcourt Ripple, and Lady Simpson with her Foxhanger Labradors, were the first to compete successfully in working trials with working gundogs and this was followed by Miss Gowland who made her F.T. Champion Foxhanger Maize up to a Working Trials Champion. This must have been a tremendous achievement in training a dog to such a high degree of perfection on both game and human scent.

Mrs Mason of the Linnifold prefix brought the present-day Labradors to the fore with her first T.D. win at the East Anglia Working Trials Training Society Championship Trials in 1963. Her bitch, Karadoc Zanella, gained 219½ marks out of 220 marks and knocked my German Shepherd W.T. Ch. Quest of Ardfern into second place with 216½ marks. We had both gained full marks in the nosework section and only a 'messy' directional control on my part separated us at the finish. That win was only the start of an era with Mrs Mason's

Labradors winning a total of thirteen Working Trials Certificates and making up three different Working Trials Champions in the space of twelve years.

The success of Mrs Mason's breeding is shown by the achievements of Susan Wood's Linnifold Black Magic (Maggi), who won the T.D. Stake at the first ever Kennel Club Working Trials Championships. I had the pleasure of judging this Stake and can only say that Maggi tracked like a vacuum cleaner and never lifted her nose from that half-mile three-hour-old track on pasture land at Enfield in England. The following year Maggi successfully defended her title by winning the second event on heather moorland at Lauder in Scotland.

Labradors from other lines of breeding have shown that their natural instinct for tracking can have an advantage over most breeds, so long as the instinct to hunt game is kept in its proper place.

Although other gundogs have shown excellent scenting abilities in working trials and obedience some of them have their limitations for control and agility work. I well remember Ian Stewart's Springer Spaniel Lawside Beauty whose little stump of a tail would show his great pleasure at tracking and he successfully completed three-hour-old tracks, but was handicapped by the agility requirements in working trials. Alex McKenzie's Springer Spaniel Tighorain Muffin Man is showing that breeds other than German Shepherds and Border Collies can take Obedience Championship Class 'C' Certificates, with sound scent discrimination to back up his superb obedience control work.

Golden Retrievers should be considered as excellent propositions for scenting work but very few seem to find their way into working trials or obedience. This is a great pity because I am sure that they could give the more popular breeds a strong challenge.

I have also watched a number of Dobermans at work in working trials, and also a few in obedience and there is no doubt in my mind that this breed needs a special kind of handler, one who has firmness, understanding and patience as a special virtue. A well handled Doberman is a sight worth watching, especially when he is working on a track or quartering the ground for a hidden criminal. When the Doberman's mind is channelled into one purposeful, constructive thought he makes all the hard work and ingenuity seem well worthwhile.

I would think that the Doberman's most loyal working supporter is Jean Faulks, of the Doberean prefix, from Aberdeen. Jean was my first ever working trials judge in 1959 and I stewarded for her last Obedience Championship Class 'C' judging appointment in 1978. During those years in between I have watched her puppies work their way up to competitive adult life. The trials and tribulations during their lengthy period of adolescence to the pride of qualifying through each stage of working trials must have given Jean a great deal of satisfaction.

Working Rottweilers in the UK are few and far between and it is therefore difficult to assess their true potential. Again I feel that this breed requires a greater understanding than most, but judging Terry Hadley's W.T. Ch. Jacinto's Bolero P.D. Ex., T.D. Ex., whilst working in a Championship T.D. Stake did make me realize just how well schooled they can be and yet independent enough to search and track with the best.

Boxers seem to have completely lost favour in the field of scent work. It may well be that breeding for show-ring requirements, without a genuine following for scent work, has diluted the natural instinct to such a degree that suitable periods of concentration are now difficult to obtain. Whatever the reason, this fine breed does not get the opportunities of years gone by.

During the late 1950s and early 1960s Anne West was able to show that Boxers could work, with Sannox Rory Dhu becoming a Working Trials Champion by winning two P.D. Working Trials Certificates. Two of her other Boxers went on to win one Working Trials Certificate each.

Standard Poodles are seldom seen around, except in the show-ring, but the occasional specimen does turn up from time to time in obedience or working trials. Their success rate in trials does show that the scenting capabilities have been retained from their ancestry of hunting dogs. The smaller and more popular varieties, however, are regular entrants at obedience shows.

Great Danes always seem to look out of place when asked to do any form of control work but I do recall judging one in a T.D. Championship Stake. This was Mr Highlife of Merrowlea owned by Mr F. Parsons of Kent. Although I was not impressed with this dog's application on the track he certainly merited his T.D.Ex. qualification.

One other very unusual breed judged in a Championship T.D. Stake was an Irish Wolfhound, Marhaba of Berryfield, owned by Miss Joan Milnes, a veterinary surgeon. Being one of the Gazehound family it is a most unlikely breed to qualify through to the top Championship Stake. Joan had trained and worked German Shepherds in the past but had rescued this bitch and took on the extremely difficult task of training her for working trials. On this occasion Marhaba worked an inch-perfect track and found all three articles, but I am sure Joan would rather forget about the search exercise where the Wolfhound's independent mind came to the fore. Nevertheless, this dog was the only one to qualify excellent from an entry of eighteen dogs. To take first prize and the coveted Working Trials Certificate was no mean achievement, especially when so many good proven dogs failed to qualify.

It had often puzzled me to understand why a sighting hunter should have such a sensitive nose and it was only Marhaba's lack of concentration which made her an inconsistent worker. However, reading *All About Gazehounds* by Joanna Russell (published by Pelham Books) brought to my notice that the Irish Wolfhound was bred in the mid-nineteenth century from the Scottish Deer Hound and the Great Dane, or in some cases the Bloodhound, to give the breed the size required. It would appear that the Bloodhound's tremendous scenting ability has been incorporated to some extent into the Wolfhound's inheritance.

Smaller breeds in the UK are at a distinct disadvantage. The Border Collie is the Queen of obedience but the small breeds have rather a limited future unless handled by an exceptionally understanding owner. Their numbers in competition are ever diminishing. Although they should all be capable of carrying out the scent discrimination exercises the precision required to progress is not quite so easily attained.

In working trials the agility tests prevent most smaller dogs from progressing beyond the U.D. Stake and some are quite unsuited for the more elementary agility tests where the tests are graded to suit the size of the dog. These restrictions certainly affect the entry of the smaller dog although we do occasionally find a handler with sufficient interest to use his dog's natural ability to the fullest the regulations will permit.

Crossbreeds and mongrels are permitted to enter both obedience shows and working trials so long as they have been suitably registered at the Kennel Club. These dogs with unacceptable or unknown parentage for full breed registration can be entered in the Obedience and Working Trials Register and can qualify through to become full Obedience or Working Trials Champions.

In the USA, however, there is no restriction caused through the size of dog. Within the obedience trials the agility requirements are controlled by the height of the dog and the tracking tests involve no other exercise. This enables all pure-bred dogs in the US to train for Utility Dog (U.D.) and Tracker Dog (T.D.) titles.

4

The Educational Process

Any educational process for a dog should be determined by the nature and extent of his inherited abilities, his limits of concentration and also his general upbringing.

These inherited abilities result from your own choice, whether by design or accident and may also depend on your purpose or choice for work or just as a family pet. A good or lucky choice can make life so much easier if we know how to capitalize on such good fortune.

Limits of concentration will vary from one dog to another and can be affected by the dog's general upbringing, the inhibitions unwittingly created by the handler's approach to control training, or to the lack of basic training.

Concentration can be relative to the dog's age. A young puppy can concentrate for only a few seconds at a time, unless he is latched to the 'milk bar' where concentration will continue until he is completely satisfied. A developing interest and the enthusiasm of a handler can prolong the concentration and the secret of any educational process is to give full satisfaction at the height of this concentration.

To have a dog tracking beyond his mental and instinctive capacity will cause a loss of concentration. To prolong a search for articles in the undergrowth beyond the limit of full concentration will mean encouragement from the handler being abandoned and replaced by enforcement. Repeated enforcement will destroy the dog's confidence and his ability will be greatly impaired. To continue a quartering exercise beyond the dog's desire to find that missing person or criminal will introduce a factor of frustration. To have a dog hunting for the correct article in scent discrimination until he stands and stares at the handler or wanders round looking for more interesting smells is the quickest road to canine boredom.

A dog's general upbringing can be a vital factor in drawing out natural abilities and extending limits of concentration, but an unsatisfactory puppyhood can also have a devastating effect by the stifling of nature's gifts to our canine companions.

A dog who is introduced to strict obedience control at too early an age may find that he lacks the confidence or initiative to carry out the various scenting applications. The handler who applies these strict controls without sufficient consideration for the effects on his dog's mental outlook will find that he is his dog's greatest handicap. Such a handler will soon lose confidence in himself and will also lack the initiative to think his way out of self-created problems.

This docs not mean that a puppy should be allowed to grow up in a completely uncontrolled state, but it does mean that the amount of obedience training and the nature of its application should be tempered to achieve a happy enthusiastic scent worker who can act responsibly with the knowledge that his handler is dependent on him.

PUPPY CHOICE AND TRAINING CONSIDERATIONS

It has been said that the puppies in the litter who are the keenest to carry bits and pieces around are the best prospects as scent workers. This may well be true. The natural instinct to carry certainly simplifies the educational process and allows more time to be devoted to other training factors, but the other puppies in the litter should not be discounted.

It is interesting to watch a litter of eight-week-old puppies being taken from their kennel and run and put in a new environment just outside their territorial home. A few may be uncertain and wish to go back into their patch, whilst others will investigate, some by sight, but in general a puppy's nose will tell him much more about his new environment. The most inquisitive puppy with the determination to sniff out every conceivable smell will probably turn out to be the best choice for scent work.

It is not intended that the general training of a puppy be

a subject of this book but the basis for our educational
process must have its foundation on an instant response to
our requirements. Older dogs who have not had the benefit
of enlightened owners and have missed out on the joy of a
controlled but exciting puppyhood will find the educational
process a little more demanding. The owners of such dogs
will find their new role as canine tutor much more interesting and rewarding, but may well find greater difficulties en
route when their dog's shortcomings are due to their own
lack of knowledge and understanding.

However, we all recognize that tutoring a dog requires
patience, understanding and enthusiasm and the earlier the
constructive educational process starts the less time will be
required to rectify earlier failings.

Most scenting applications require a sound recall and
retrieve as a foundation before we can proceed with the
more serious stages of training. Although tracking can be the
exception there seems to be little value in spending time and
effort building up a first-rate tracker if he will not come back
to his handler when called during his off-duty periods and it
is also doubtful if any scent working dog can achieve the full
enjoyment in life if he cannot retrieve.

Control training, discussed in the next chapter, is therefore
based on the competition requirements for the retrieve
exercise in obedience shows. Handlers who are interested in
working trials will require to follow the same procedure, but
the owner of the family pet who only wishes to broaden the
enjoyment of his dog without the competitive requirements
can ignore certain elements of the exercise but should not
attempt to take short cuts through the basic principles.

INDUCEMENTS AND ENTHUSIASM
The foundation of all educational processes comes down to
the enthusiastic application of inducements.

As human beings, we can all work hard if the 'carrot' is
big enough and within our reach, especially if we have the
enthusiastic backing of friends and family. If the rewards or
benefits are not very big we may not put much effort into a
project. If it is going to take too long to achieve our aims we

may not be able to sustain the initial momentum and some people require greater inducement and enthusiastic encouragement than others to become fully motivated.

Some people work with fear as the inducement, but individuals in this category usually require constant supervision, they lack consistency and initiative and they cannot give of their best. Fear can often prevent a person from carrying out a function of which he is perfectly capable, or confuse him to a degree that he will clutch at any straw to avoid the tyranny of his oppressor.

I do not think the basic philosophy of the canine educational process is any different. Dogs require inducements and enthusiastic encouragement, but they do not have the understanding of a human being and the approach must be simple with the inducement of an obvious reward.

The inducement of fear is often used by many dog trainers, and some say that a dog cannot be trained without the application of fear. There are times when a certain amount of firmness must be applied and this can cause a degree of canine apprehension, but this only indicates our lack of knowledge or ability to achieve the objective by more constructive means.

Inducements can be placed into two categories and should be classified as PRIMARY and SECONDARY.

A *primary* inducement is an activity a dog understands and desires prior to and during the particular function being carried out. This is a very important introduction to the training of any scent work exercise and so a very useful introduction to most control training.

A *secondary* inducement is an activity which, from past experience, has led the dog to understand that a pleasant reward will result from his action.

If, for example, normally your dog is fed in the kitchen, but you have decided that feeding him in the garden would be more appropriate, you would make up his meal in the kitchen as usual and let him know that you are taking it outside and encourage him to come with you. His food being a *primary* inducement would take him out to the garden with you. Repeat this process for two or three days and he will be out ahead of you and waiting at his new feeding area.

After this procedure has been established he could then be shut in the kitchen whilst his meal was placed outside in its regular place. The opening of the kitchen door would release him to head directly to his feeding area; past experience has told him his food will be there, the food has now become a *secondary* inducement.

If the *primary* inducement had not been utilized most dogs would have taken longer to realize there was a direct route from the kitchen to the new feeding area.

Using the same principle, the family pet can be taught to find the children. If he is taken to a position within sight and sound of them he will want to go and play with them. He can then be released with encouragement to 'go and find them'. Repeating the process would soon make him keen to go when he was within earshot of the children. By means of encouragement to 'go and find them' each time he is released from a greater distance, the pattern would become established with great desire to find the children without sight or sound of them. The joy of finding, from past experience, would become the *secondary* inducement which would sustain this enthusiastic activity.

Take away this *secondary* inducement and send him out for a few consecutive excursions when the children are not there and he will soon become disillusioned. He will have no incentive to continue the exercise and the value of the previous inducements will have been lost.

A policeman and his fully trained tracking dog will have their failures, and they are not necessarily the dog's fault. Too many failures and the dog will lose confidence in himself and his handler. The inducement to track can be lost.

My house is on the outskirts of a small Scottish town with a field adjoining my garden at the rear of the house, an ideal spot for a burglary on a dark night. We were the victims one evening whilst out shopping. Jeza, our only dog at the time, was with us in the car. The intruders broke the dining-room window catches for a means of entry.

With this forced entry at the back of the house and an adjoining field with a farm track some hundred yards away, it was apparent to the police and to me that the intruders had come and gone by that route. The local police dog was called in but, under ideal conditions, could not locate any track. The dog worked, and worked very hard, but could not find any trace of a track.

Police enquiries later revealed that the intruders had driven to the front of the house in a motor car and were never in the field which had been so closely scrutinized by the tracker dog. This complete failure could not be explained to the tracker dog and more incidents like it would ruin his confidence.

The prime inducement to a fully experienced tracking dog is the sheer joy of tracking and the praise for doing it so well. The failure to start a track because of outside circumstances must be countered by success and it is common to hear of a policeman giving his dog a nice easy training track after such a failure. This track is generally known as a 'sweetener'. It is aptly named as the enjoyment and pleasure of such a track will act as a *secondary* inducement the next time an operational track is called for. Without those 'sweeteners' the operational police tracker dog would become too confused to be of much real value.

As all dogs vary in character, intelligence and inherited instincts, different types and strengths of inducement must be considered for each dog. Some dogs find long periods of concentration quite impossible, but the correct approach for these dogs may well break down the barrier and create canine enthusiasm well beyond the expectation for that particular breed. Others with very limited inherited interest for a particular scenting application may never be motivated beyond a very elementary stage.

TRAINING ELEMENTS
Every control exercise or scenting application can be broken down into elements with some being temporarily changed to facilitate the correct inducements and to achieve the pattern of behaviour required.

If we ask a dog to search for a missing article, how is he to know what we want? When he finds the article, how does he know what to do with it? Do we ask him to stand over the article or do we expect him to return with it? He cannot know what is being requested unless we take the time and trouble to guide him through each training element.

Each control exercise and scenting application should be broken down into elements, analysed for order of introduction into the educational process and modified if required to achieve a smooth flow from one element to another. Certain activities which are decidedly wrong in the latter stages of the educational process may be necessary as an inducement at the introductory stage.

When handlers watch dogs execute a particular scenting application at an obedience show or working trials, they may observe a number of good dogs carrying out a superbly controlled scent discrimination or a beautifully executed search. Some handlers then go back to their training club, set up the test to the competition requirements and expect their dogs to perform adequately. Unfortunately, a few dogs have sufficient intelligence to perform adequately in spite of their handlers, but without the proper foundation the handlers of these dogs do not have the knowledge to achieve an improvement in this initial standard. The dogs become pressurized by impatient handlers and they break, with less than adequate performances becoming the order of the day.

Some dogs are natural-born trackers and give their inexperienced handlers success after success. Then the dog has a failure, the reason is probably unknown and may not have been the fault of the dog, the handler is lost, he does not know what action to take. An incorrect analysis with a forceful 'no nonsense' attitude from the handler can create another failure. The dog becomes confused and failures appear as often as the earlier successes. Another dog has become the victim of human failure.

However, the systematic breaking down of every scenting application and a full understanding of each element can go a long way to minimizing failures. This can give a handler the knowledge and ability to recognize and eliminate the causes of failure.

DIFFERENCES FROM ONE DOG TO ANOTHER
No two dogs are the same in character, temperament or inherited instinct. Even within a single breed the variation can be quite remarkable and the upbringing and home life can make such differences in two similar puppies from the same nest. The character and outlook of every human being is the result of a multitude of varying circumstances, the same is true of every dog.

Two dogs of similar intelligence can progress at differing rates. Compound this variation by using a different trainer for each dog and we shall find that the difference in progress widens. Some elements may seem very easy for one partnership whereas other elements prove to be much more difficult, yet the reverse can be true of a different partnership.

Again different breeds mature at varying ages. Many people in the competitive field will go for a Border Collie because serious training can be started at a relatively early age and so many elements fall into place so readily. On the other hand the Doberman has the reputation of having years of adolescence where great patience is advised until maturity achieves the stability required for more advanced training.

However, an easily trained dog does not necessarily indicate an expert handler. The novice handler who finds that everything comes easily may not have the understanding or ability to cope with a problem when it arises. He may also have based his training approach on the wrong principles and created more complex problems at a much later date, problems which may fail to indicate their source to the closed mind of the handler who created them. Some dogs, especially Border Collies, can accept a fair amount of mishandling and rough treatment, but where this happens these conditions eventually take their toll on this willing and loyal breed. Dogs who receive such treatment eventually become confused and fail to understand the simplest of requirements. The handlers of these confused dogs generally fail to realize the cause and continue to mishandle and compound the confusion with distressing results.

THE ART OF UNDERSTANDING

The prevention of faults is not always possible. Dogs are not bred with a complete understanding of human thoughts and sentiments and we seem to be even less well endowed with understanding of the canine mind.

Failures in industry, commerce and even our private lives are often due to a lack of understanding or appreciation between people who are in a position to communicate in the same language. People who are born with similar instincts and are brought up with the same moral code do not always interpret the same meaning from a discussion or an instruction. How can we, as imperfect mortals, expect our canine friends to interpret all our requirements or instructions unless we are prepared to study a dog's limitations as well as our own, understand his needs and instincts and appreciate his moods or desires?

Many training methods are based on years of other people's experiences. Most methods are very sound, but our limitations are often evident by the time it can take us to realize that a mistake has been made. As we all tend to develop personal variations of the accepted methods and consider them to be more suitable than the original approach, we sometimes find it difficult to accept that a particular variation, or our execution of it, can be the cause of a problem. Personal pride can, at times, become a handicap.

However, an early appreciation of a developing fault can help to prevent a major problem and handlers should always be aware that a single adverse response, once repeated, is likely to become a habit.

TRAINING PROGRAMMES

One reads from time to time of regimented training programmes or handlers with short-term target dates for the completion of a particular stage in training. This may look good on paper or sound fine in discussion and in experienced hands they may work out, but dogs being what they are and handlers being even less predictable, failure to maintain a set programme is usually due to our inability to appreciate that our canine companions have not as yet been computerized.

A programme with flexibility is certainly worthwhile, a programme based on results is more than commendable. A programme which defines the most likely sequence of training elements for the various exercises, one which can be modified in the light of experience, progress or hold-ups will guarantee the easiest and quickest road to success.

To skimp a training element to meet a specific date – there may be a show or trials due – is likely to cause long-term problems, especially if success is achieved at the event. This is likely to give the handler the impression that short cuts are worthwhile.

To enter a show or trials for the purpose of assessing progress or to gain experience can be worthwhile, but can also be damaging if the dog gets the opportunity of realizing there is a wrong way as well as a right one.

A flexible training programme tailored to suit the particular dog can, however, give a handler an incentive to work and reason for pride when the long-term objectives have been achieved.

5
Basic Control

Every dog should know the meaning of control and any dog who has the advantage of his owner's interest in scenting applications can only benefit from that interest if his education has been based on a smart recall and an enjoyable retrieve. The requirements for competition work, whether working trials or obedience competitions, do entail further development to comply with essential conditions of the RECALL and RETRIEVE exercises, but this chapter will consider primarily the approach to achieve a happy and consistent response to the basic purpose of the exercises. The chapter will then continue with further development to bring in the finer points required for competition objectives.

The Recall – To obtain a dog's instant attention at any distance with the immediate response of returning directly to his handler.

The Retrieve – The dog to go out immediately on release, pick up the article in question and return directly to the handler and present the article to hand.

The training for a sound retrieve is controlled, to a great extent, by the progress of the recall. A healthy recall is essential before freedom in retrieving can be considered. As both functions are directly related, the programming of each training element should be timed to ensure that the progress of the recall function is used to achieve an unimpaired retrieving schedule.

THE RECALL
A number of dogs will respond quite naturally to a recall, they have a built-in desire to please and have a handler with the ability to capitalize on their virtue. Other dogs have a

very strong streak of independence bred into them and require very understanding handling to maintain a sensible relationship with their handler.

Some breeds are easy and some are difficult, some respond keenly to the recall from a very early age and other breeds can be very trying until they reach maturity. Unfortunately, faulty handling can ensure that maturity is just the continuation of a problematic adolescence.

The shepherding breeds which still have a strong working instinct are probably the most responsive on the recall with the Dobermans, as mentioned before, requiring a special kind of understanding until they reach maturity. Gundogs in general are usually responsive but members of the Setter family, who seem to love the freedom of the open space, can prove to be rather exasperating for an inexperienced handler once they have tasted complete freedom.

An understanding of a dog's reluctance to conform is very important, but that understanding does not necessarily mean the acceptance of a defiant attitude. It does mean, however, that each handler should recognize the probable causes and his responsibility to counter them. Preventing a problem is always more satisfying and less time consuming than trying to repair damage already done.

A puppy should not require any formal training to come when called, but a dog of any age should have a genuine desire to be with his handler. There should be something to come back for, something much more interesting than the thought taking his attention when called. There must be a reason for doing what is asked of him; the reason may be love and affection creating respect, it may be the knowledge that fun and games will result from his instant response to the call or it may be the expectation of a nice juicy titbit. Whatever it is, he should think it worthwhile.

The two significant factors controlling the response to return when called are:

1. Conflict of interests
2. Distance between dog and handler

The conflict of interests can vary tremendously and may well be the greatest cause of defiance and refusal to respond promptly to the call. A short distance between dog and handler can weaken that defiance by the knowledge that he will not get away with it, but a greater distance can strengthen the defiance by the dog's realization that he can run faster than his human companion and he may well enjoy the chase. Any punishment after his capture or belated voluntary return will not be related in the dog's mind to his failure to respond in the first place, but it will be considered as a very unpleasant experience at the hands of his master for the latest event in his mind — that of returning. He may have been cornered and will be more cunning the next time, he will not wish to experience the wrath of his master. If he has finally returned voluntarily and received punishment he will be more apprehensive next time. A succession of such events will finally implant the unpleasantness in the dog's mind to such an extent that he will always be reluctant to return.

If a dog has found an attractive smell his interest may well exceed the handler's control for an immediate response. If he has found a bitch with amorous inclinations a real problem has developed with a great conflict of interests. If two male dogs start squaring up to each other, neither will wish to back down and very effective handler control will be required if a dog is going to show any sign of weakness by turning his back and walking away from his adversary. There are times when the conflict of interests is so great that it can be good policy to go up to the dog and prevent this conflict by putting him on the lead and abandoning the thought of recalling under these particular circumstances.

Each situation should be fully assessed and the dog recalled only when a favourable response is expected. Otherwise the situation should be created where immediate attention and a willing recall is guaranteed.

Young puppies can be conditioned from the start to be responsive to their names by making use of their natural curiosity. This can be done by giving a little tap or flick on the hindquarters with a finger as the dog is walking away with nothing special on his mind. At the same time call his name and curiosity will make him turn his head to see what is wanted. He may only be about a couple of feet away, but call him in and make a great fuss of him. The inducement to come back when called can be a ball to play with, something tasty to eat or just a little affection; whatever it is he must feel that it is worthwhile.

When you are happy with his response allow a little more distance between yourself and your puppy. Do not call him if his attention is fixed on something; a conflict of interest should be left until he is fully responsive to the call — when little appears to be on his mind. At the same time take advantage of natural situations when the puppy or older dog is coming to you of his own free will. Whilst he is coming to you call him in and make a great fuss of the event.

Commands are not necessary, although it depends on one's interpretation of the word. One definition from the dictionary is 'to exercise supreme authority over': this interpretation will never achieve the desired happy response. However, if the definition is 'to influence', the dog may recognize this as a much more pleasant approach.

Some of the more independent breeds may well respond as puppies to the approach just described but adolescence and maturity may bring a streak of defiance to the fore where a conflict of interests can rear its ugly head. This situation must be recognized immediately to prevent defiance, through independence, from developing into a way of life.

A defiant dog can show this trait in a number of ways and as already stated it may well be due to handler failing rather than the dog's natural stubbornness. The dog may ignore his handler's call completely as if he were deaf, he may run away expecting to be chased, he may come running back until he is almost within reach then run away, or he may carry on and run right past. Whatever causes the problem it can become exasperating and will take a less understanding handler beyond the limits of a reasonable reaction.

The secret of a sound, instant response to the handler's call is never to be in a position where the dog is likely to refuse and defy his handler. If you expect a refusal, do not call, deploy yourself into a position where refusal is extremely unlikely or wait for the correct moment. Create success and avoid failures.

To overcome such defiant problems or to prevent them it is advisable to consolidate on the puppy conditioning approach with the use of a slip chain and a good long lead, say five to seven feet in length, to bring in the training element which overcomes the conflict of interest situations.

This training element is the basis for an instant response to the call at any time. The preconditioned puppy will respond very quickly, but the defiant creature will take some time to realize that he must respond immediately every time and much ground work may be required to ensure success.

Take the dog on the lead and just walk, do not apply any control and let your dog do just what he wants. If he pulls just let him, or if he stops to sniff let him. When you are ready, call his name as you give a sharp tug on the lead, move back and away from him calling him to you with urgency and enthusiasm, create a real desire to be with you. Any harshness in the voice should be only in the use of his name to obtain instant attention and this must be followed immediately by the encouraging call to come.

The preconditioned puppy will become very attentive and will watch the handler's every move after a minimal period. Good timing and a sensible application of the slip chain and lead will also have a remarkable effect on the more defiant dog, but it will take much longer to consolidate and be sure of the desired response every time.

This process can be continued with the use of a long line. The more responsive dog should not need to be subjected to this process but guaranteed success is more important than discarding this option. A line of fifteen to twenty feet in length should be sufficient. A strong cord may do and it is preferable to avoid the type of line likely to be used for tracking. The best tracking lines are made of waxed cotton, the type obtained as a good quality clothes line or window sash cord.

The application of the long line is identical to that of the lead. Again give the dog plenty of freedom to do what he wants, if necessary create distance between yourself and the dog. Allow him to take an interest in something of his own choice then call him. Do not accept a negative response.

Failure to respond on the first call will necessitate positive and immediate action. A further call should coincide with a sharp tug on the line. Use enthusiasm and urgency in your voice and any movements to ensure that he comes back to you quickly. If necessary move back at speed to draw him to you quicker. Never move towards your dog when you call him, this will only slow him down.

Do not forget to praise him, he must enjoy coming back to you. Do not be too ready to discard the line. Let your dog drag it around for some time and be sure he comes in at every call, no matter where you are or what he is doing. Only ten consecutive successes can give a handler confidence in the result of the eleventh.

THE RETRIEVE

The Principles
If all dogs could have the carrying instinct of the working Labradors, Golden Retrievers and Spaniels, dog training would be so much simpler. They seem to be the most natural dogs for carrying and delivering to hand. No gamekeeper is going to waste his time teaching a dog to bring to hand if he can breed from 'natural' stock.

To pick up and carry is the most natural action for any dog. How else could he take a treasured bone to bed? In days gone by, a dog would carry excess food and bury it for another meal.

An example of this comes to mind with Jeza, our German Shepherd, who was six months old when she joined our family and on the first day in her new home gave us a very enlightening experience. Obviously she felt rather strange and when presented with her first meal she was more concerned about her change of environment than satisfying her inner self. However, something told her that she might not be offered another meal so, bit by bit, she picked out the pieces of meat and buried them in every corner she could find in the garden. She could carry the pieces of meat because nature told her and yet it took almost twelve months to teach her the retrieve exercise to a competitive standard.

There is a big difference between having a dog who will pick up and carry and one who will bring to hand. Although it is natural for a dog to carry when he sees the need it is not so natural to give. The instinct to carry is the instinct to keep and dogs in the wild soon learn to be protective over their possessions. The domestic canine companions, however, learn that their human friends are prepared to share and will give to hand when they fully understand that this is part of an enjoyable game.

A puppy tossing a ball in the air on his own might be imagining that it is a live mouse and he is having fun with it before the final kill. Or a terrier fighting and shaking a slipper to the death might well be thinking of a cornered and captured rodent. No wonder we have so many problems when we expect a dog to return immediately he has the retrieved article in his mouth.

It is easy to develop retrieving faults and at times difficult to appreciate their existence until they have a good hold. However, the full understanding of retrieve training is held within the RETRIEVE MATRIX and this is based on two of the principal canine traits, those of POSSESSIVENESS and SUBMISSIVENESS.

Each dog has his natural level of either trait, from very strong in some dogs to very weak in others. It is the combination of these strengths which govern our progress in retrieve training.

A strong *possessive* trait should result in a dog having a very keen natural desire to go after a ball or other suitable article. However, a dog who is weak in this trait will require to be suitably induced to realize the pleasures of controlled possessiveness.

A strong *submissive* trait will result in an easy recall unless unsympathetic handling has created apprehension or fear and the negation of a natural response. A weak submissive trait will undoubtedly result in a very independent dog unless this factor is properly controlled.

Therefore, we have four combinations within the MATRIX to give us a variety of basic training situations. (See Figure 1).

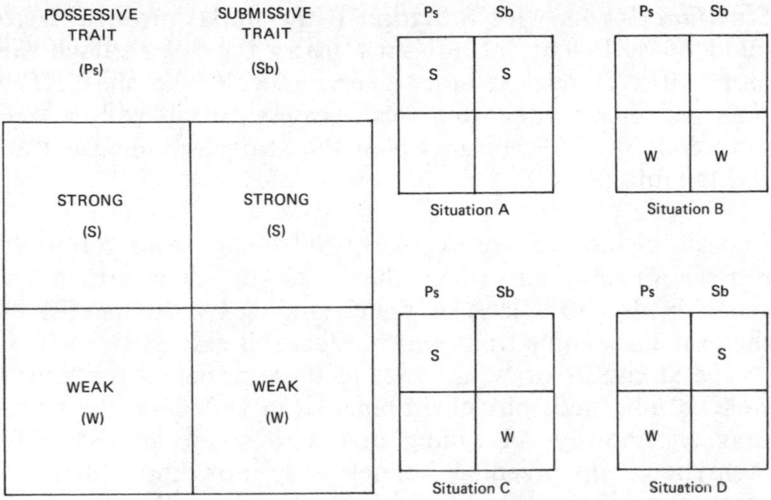

POSSESSIVE TRAIT (Ps)	SUBMISSIVE TRAIT (Sb)
STRONG (S)	STRONG (S)
WEAK (W)	WEAK (W)

Ps Sb

S	S

Situation A

Ps Sb

W	W

Situation B

Ps Sb

S	
	W

Situation C

Ps Sb

	S
W	

Situation D

Fig. 1 The retrieve matrix.

Situation A   The combination of two strong traits creates the easiest training conditions where the strong possessive trait ensures a natural desire to go out and take possession of the article and the strong submissive trait ensures an immediate return on the call.

Situation B   This combination of two weak traits will create a situation where great patience will be required with the timing and introduction of each training element being controlled to assure success. Here we have a dog with no desire to go out for the article and when he has been induced to go out will become too independent to return unless the handler has overcome the 'conflict of interests' situation.

Situation C   The strength of possessiveness will achieve an enthusiastic run out for the article and simplify the initial training but the problems in handling the uncontrolled independent dog require to be tackled and cured before any further progress can be made. The failure to recognize this situation is often witnessed when a dog can be seen to run out for a thrown article and then run away to find his own form of amusement with his toy.

Situation D   As with Situation B the initial problem is to build up sufficient enthusiasm to carry the dog through the more difficult retrieve-based exercises which lie ahead. The time and effort put into a weak possessive trait will be well rewarded by the ease in which the strong submissive trait will fall into place.

The problems we see regularly with dogs who refuse to retrieve or play up when they pick up their article are generally due to a lack of understanding by the handler of the principal canine traits which affect this exercise.

The strengths or weaknesses of these principal traits may well be inherited, but environment can influence the situation enormously. A young dog who spent an extended puppyhood in breeding kennels may not know how to enjoy the fun and games which can be had with toys of his own, especially when the owner is not prepared to play with him. A forced method used in the early stages of training can give the impression of weakness instead of a strong possessive trait. There can be many man-made reasons for failing to achieve a happy and responsive retrieving dog.

Man-made reasons for retrieving failures can be more difficult and time consuming to rectify than a straight forward programme used to train a dog from scratch.

A Training Technique
Before asking a dog to retrieve and give to hand he must be sound on the recall, he must also be capable and reliable at picking up, holding and carrying the article then releasing it into your hand when asked.

The recall element has already been covered in this chapter but the full breakdown of training elements can be given:
1. Take, hold, then carry the article.
2. Pick up and present to hand.
3. Go out, pick up and return.

Many puppies are happy to take an article from their handler and carry it around, but quite a number of puppies become troublesome because a foreceful approach has been applied to make the youngster return and give the article to hand. Puppies or dogs with this natural aptitude should be coaxed along to carry and have fun but never asked to return with the article until the recall has been consolidated, to avoid a 'clash of interests'.

The same basic approach for retrieve training can be applied to dogs of all breeds but progress through the various stages will differ tremendously. Some dogs with the most advantageous strength of the principal traits, the most suitable upbringing and an intelligent handler can accomplish the objective with the minimum training. Others who are not so fortunate may seem to take a lifetime.

1. Take, Hold, then Carry the Article The article to be used during the initial training of this element is your index finger. Any puppy or dog should become familiar with your finger massaging his gums and be quite happy to accept your finger in his mouth. No owner is worthy of a dog if he cannot carry out this function without being bitten.

With your dog sitting, straddle him so that you are both facing in the same direction, show your affection by stroking his cheeks and place your index finger behind his canines. With your thumb over his muzzle and remaining fingers under his lower jaw hold his mouth shut. Give gentle praise, stroke his cheek and ask him to 'Hold', but restrict this action to about three or four seconds during the first few occasions. Do not overdo it and do not lengthen the holding periods until he is happy to accept this procedure.

You are always in a position to know if there is any loose skin from the upper or lower lips being caught between the finger and the dog's teeth and this should be released before any pressure is applied. Any attempt to apply excessive pressure when holding the dog's muzzle will hurt you long before it has any effect on your dog. When you wish to remove your finger release your grip over his muzzle and, as he opens his mouth to release the index finger, ask him to 'Give'.

It will not take him long to realize that your index finger behind his canines is quite an acceptable experience and he will hold without any pressure being applied to keep his mouth shut. Each time you put your finger in his mouth use a gentle 'Hold' as you praise and stroke him. Make sure the experience becomes a pleasant one but be ready to hold his mouth shut if he thinks of opening it before you ask him to give your finger back.

When you are perfectly happy with your dog's acceptance of this procedure prepare to teach him to carry your finger. Stand in front of your dog (he may be sitting or standing) and get him to hold your index finger again. With your thumb over his muzzle and the remaining fingers under his lower jaw encourage him to walk with you as you move backwards. Keep asking him to hold, encourage him and on occasions pull against his canines but make sure he does not open his mouth. Let him release your finger only when you are ready and request it.

It is the sensitivity of your own finger which prevents you from applying excess pressure when holding your dog's mouth shut and this ensures a gentle, considerate approach to the rudiments of retrieve training.

During this period of training you are in a position to control your dog's actions. If he is going to reject your finger you have the means of preventing it. You will be able to sense his actions much quicker than if using some other object. You are in a position to comfort by stroking his cheeks and yet apply the correct amount of pressure as and when it is required with the knowledge that you cannot be hurting him.

Progress depends to a great extent on your approach and the dog's readiness to accept your actions. Dogs who have already been trained to retrieve but have mouthing problems or are reluctant to release the article can be retrained by using this method.

The next stage is to use a suitable replacement for your index finger. A half-inch diameter piece of wooden dowelling is probably the answer. Again it is preferable to straddle your dog so that you are both facing the same direction and put the article in his mouth whilst you ask him to hold it. Praise and stroking his cheeks will help to dispel any anxiety.

You will probably find that he will accept the change of 'article' and prove that the groundwork with your index finger has been worthwhile. You can then stand in front of him and with one hand under his chin get him to follow as you move backwards. It will be realized by the owners of small dogs that they will need to get down to the dog's level and instead of standing straddled over the dog they may have to kneel. Dogs can respond much better when people are down to their level and the basic training can be carried out from the kneeling position. Although this should not cause any problems the next stage can be rather difficult and it may well be more suitable to make the change from the finger to another article whilst kneeling straddled over the dog.

Keep the training sessions short and make sure he does not get bored. It should not take him long to realize there is great pleasure in strutting round with an article in his mouth.

When you have full confidence that your dog wants to walk around holding the article run away and call him to you. Get him excited but prepare to use a firm 'Hold' if he thinks of mouthing, chewing or even dropping the article. You may wish to carry out the initial part of this training whilst the dog is on the lead.

It is only when he holds with excitement that you can consider enticing him to take the article from you as you tease him with it. Having done this successfully on a few occasions you can 'accidentally' drop the article as he tries to grab it from you. In the excitement he should be ready to pick up the article and carry it as you induce the recall whilst moving away from him.

This is a critical stage in the training programme and it is important that he picks up from the 'accidental' drop before progressing to the next element.

2. Pick up and present to hand The pick up should now be consolidated by dropping the article and on occasions by kicking it around to increase the dog's desire to get hold of it.

As he has been taught to hold and carry until you take the article from him there should not be any problems in getting him to present to hand although the excitement may have made your dog forget. If this happens it may be good policy to put him on the lead for a short spell to bring his mind back to the initial recall training element. Again one hundred per cent success is required before considering instructions to go out and fetch.

3. Go out, pick up and return   The sight of the training article should now be sufficient to excite your dog and a short throw can be tried. Dogs with a strong response to the recall may find the excitement of a longer throw more to their liking. As soon as the dog picks up the article, revert to the recall procedure as you move backwards to bring him back as fast as possible.

Verbal instructions to 'Fetch it' are not necessary at this juncture. It is the desire to get the article which takes the dog out and not the command. The use of verbal instructions at this stage can result in a commanding voice which may put the dog off. When the verbal instruction is used it should be in the form of an excited request rather than a formal command. He can then learn the meaning of the phrase 'Fetch it' after he knows how to perform the act. A command, instruction or request verbally given to a dog means nothing until he knows how to perform the act.

When the pick up, hold, carry and deliver to hand is to your satisfaction the extended throw can now be developed so that your dog will go out any distance to pick up and return to you.

The same enthusiasm can be generated to develop the desire to go out and fetch any type of article. Note the types of article your dog does not favour; many dogs do not like picking up metal, and it is best to avoid such articles until the retrieve has been fully consolidated.

THE FINER POINTS
Your dog now knows to come immediately he is called and will run out and retrieve a variety of articles for you, but to accommodate the competition requirements for scent dis-crimination it is advisable that he be taught the full competitive retrieve exercise.

This means that your dog must remain sitting by your side

as you throw an article and then go out when instructed, return with the article, sit in front of you whilst you take the article from him and then finish round to heel when told.

Certain of the finer points should be taught without the use of articles and be treated initially as elements of the recall. Each element can then be combined to complete the sequence of events which make up the full retrieve exercise. The remaining elements are:
1.   Sit square in front of the handler when called in.
2.   Smartly round to heel to finish the exercise.
3.   The controlled retrieve.

1.   Sit nice and square   Teaching a dog to sit nice and square in front of you will require a return to the initial recall training with slip chain and lead. Your dog will know the routine of watching you as you move around and should be attentive enough to watch and move with you as you move backwards. If you have taught him to sit quite independently then the instruction can be given as soon as he is close in front of you. To hold his attention high, looking up at your face, will help to induce an automatic sit. Teaching the sit for titbits can be extremely useful.

When teaching your dog to sit in front without the inducement of food place one hand under his lower jaw and lift his head, at the same time press with your other hand on his croup. Whilst he is moving into the sit position give him an abundance of praise. When your dog accepts this procedure willingly he will anticipate the movement and will sit without the need to touch him. He will eventually realize that he should sit when called in as part of the recall or retrieve exercise.

2. Smartly to heel   This element should not be attempted until you are perfectly happy with the 'sit in front' and it is advisable to use a slip chain and lead.

The early stages of training are best accomplished by making most of the movement yourself. With the dog sitting in front of you take a step to the left and forward so that the dog is to your right and slightly behind you. Transfer your lead round your back from right to left hand and encourage your dog into your left hand side as you carry on walking a little further, until you have full control. Then make him sit nice and straight at your side with a little left hand pressure on his croup. Encouragement and praise with the already understood instruction to sit will soon dispel any anxiety. Continue at this stage until it becomes a fully accepted pattern; only then do you start reducing your own movement until the dog is completing the full manoeuvre without any assistance.

With the sit in front and finish to heel perfected on the recall, there should not be any problem when introducing an article and completing the freedom of the retrieve with a proper finish. It is important, however, not to make any corrections to these finer points whilst retrieving but return to recall training without a retrieve article until the problem is sorted out.

3. The controlled retrieve The final element now required to complete the retrieve exercise is to teach your dog to sit by your left hand side and wait for the release to go out for your thrown article. Your attitude to date has been to create enthusiasm and anticipation, he has been allowed to run free when you have thrown the article, now you want to have your dog wait for the word to go. You wish to curb his anticipation without adversely affecting his enthusiasm.

Physical restraint is now necessary. Hold his slip chain whilst you throw his article out. Keep him with you for a few seconds before releasing him with the verbal request to 'Fetch it'. When you are sure that none of the enthusiasm is lost, in fact it may get stronger, make him sit whilst you hold his slip chain and throw the article out. Keep him sitting for a few seconds before releasing him with the request to 'Fetch it'.

When he has steadied down and is ready to wait for the release to go and fetch his article, attach a cord loop to his slip chain — not to the ring, you do not wish to use it as a 'choke'. With a finger in this loop (seven to nine inches of cord will do) your dog will not know whether you can maintain physical control or not until he tries to make a break for the article.

It may well be necessary to use strong verbal commands to 'Stay' until you are prepared to release him with 'Fetch it'. This will take time, but the perfecting of any exercise takes a little time and at this stage you are having to counter your previously encouraged anticipation.

You should now have a dog fully trained in the basic exercises which are so essential to a good noseworking dog.

6

An Introduction to Scenting Theories

Scents and a dog's ability to differentiate between such a variety of scents is very much a mystery. We may have our theories, the results of various experiments, or we may have analysed the products of an intensive study on the subject, but in the end we are left with theories and little more.

Only the dog knows what scent or odour he is following on a track, or the difference between one person's scent and another when he is discriminating between articles which have been handled by different people. If a dog loses a track or fails to discriminate, who are we to censure him for an inferior performance without an understanding of the cause?

This chapter will define a number of theories: some with substantial backing from the experience of many people, others a shot in the dark based on logical thinking. Although, as yet, we do not seem to know the logic or development of the various scent patterns.

I suppose that the various scents can be broken down into three basic types and there will generally be a mixture of these around. They are:

1. Animal scents
2. Ground odours
3. Material odours

To the human scenting organs there seems to be difficulty in recognizing the presence of more than one scent source at any particular time. The scent of new-mown grass will mask all others. The aroma from bacon frying in a pan obliterates all others and the odour from disturbed farmyard manure extinguishes the many other scents from our olfactory organs. We seem to be quite incapable of appreciating anything other than the most dominant scent at any one particular time.

It would seem, however, that the canine olfactory system is capable of concentrating on scents or odours other than the dominating scent in any particular set of conditions.

I have watched dogs track across fields with newly scattered farmyard manure when the odour was rather nauseating to the human nose and yet the dogs were quite oblivious to its presence as they concentrated on the scent which we as human beings could never hope to distinguish.

I tend to consider canine scenting and human powers of vision to be on a similar level. We can see any number of objects at one time and can then focus on one item and follow its course. At the same time we can visually monitor the surrounding objects. Ability and training can help to determine our powers of general observation, even when we are concentrating on an individual item.

Our canine friends seem to have the same power in the form of scent focusing. It would appear that they can be well aware of many scents or odours whilst concentrating on one. They seem to be able to ignore dominant odours whilst giving their full attention to particular subordinate scents.

It is this ability to focus on a single subordinate scent or a particular combination of scents and odours which makes a dog of unique value to man.

ANIMAL SCENTS

We can start by considering animal scent, and in a book of this nature our main interest is in the scent of the human being, although other animal scents cannot be ignored.

When we ask a dog to track he is expected to follow the scent path created by the various personal scents and ground odours left behind by a person having walked across a piece of ground. He is not being asked to follow the scent of a particular person but of the last person to be in the particular area where he began to track. Once he has located the track he is expected to maintain contact and not transfer to another, either more recent or older than the one he decided to follow.

A dog being asked to quarter the ground for a missing person or a criminal is expected to indicate the presence and location of any human being in the area without the need to discriminate between one person and another.

A dog who is expected to apply the art of scent discrimination is given the scent from a particular person and he should indicate an article containing that person's scent from a collection of articles contaminated with the scent from various other people.

So conditioned are we to the success of a well-trained dog in the art of scent discrimination we seem to feel that the occasional failure from these experts is due to one of a number of theoretical causes. However, there is one possible cause which seems to be ignored.

In theory every person carries a distinctive scent of his or her own and this scent is basically a result of perspiration. Like fingerprints, each scent is unique to each individual and with a population of fifty million people in the UK there must be fifty million different distinctive sets of fingerprints and human scents.

A fingerprint expert in his attempt to match prints may well discard the majority with ease but can require time and all his expert training to determine the exact similarity between matching sets. With fifty million human scents, is it not possible that there are occasions when scents of two people are so similar that any slight masking by surrounding odours can negate the difference so that they appear to be the same?

Fingerprint records are grouped with each section containing basic similarities in the same manner that other human characteristics can be grouped, for example each one of us falls into a particular blood group. If necessary the same sort of classification can be done with height, the colour of a person's hair or eyes, or for that matter any other human characteristic. It is, therefore, more than probable that human scents can be classified and with the knowledge we could well find that scent is related to more obvious physical properties of the human being, such as blood or saliva groups.

Comparing scents from different classifications will no doubt be a simple exercise for any self-respecting dog and the discrimination of scents within a classification may not be too difficult unless they are very similar. Some scent classifications may well be tied within a very narrow band, thereby creating major problems for a dog lacking in the expertise or concentration necessary for the very finest discrimination of scents.

This is thought well worthy of consideration and greater depth will be given to this theory in Chapter 9, relating to the training for the scent discrimination exercise.

GROUND ODOURS

The effect of odours from vegetation can be of major importance when we come to discuss the art of tracking and we may even find that it has an effect on the scent discrimination exercise at open air obedience shows.

Walking across a piece of ground disturbs the surface to some extent and there is no doubt that any sign of vegetation affects the strength of the track odour. Bruised vegetation appears to emit relatively strong odours and it would seem that these odours change through the chemical reactions at varying times and under differing conditions.

Each different type of vegetation will have its own particular odour, and this odour will vary in accordance with the stage of growth. Vegetation full of growth in the spring will maintain a high concentration of odour when released by the effect of feet treading on the surface and crushing or bruising it. In the late autumn when the growth has well passed its peak the vegetation will be drying out and this concentration of odour will be less dominant but will still be strongest in the immediate area of any footprints.

MATERIAL ODOURS

This can generally be taken to mean any matter not directly related to the two previously discussed origins. It can relate to the articles of clothing being worn, either of man-made fibres or of an animal base. Or it can relate to articles left on a track or used for searching or scent discrimination.

Although each material will emit its own odour it will harbour human scents after being in contact with a person. A porous material will hold a human scent for some considerable time, whereas non-porous materials such as metals and some plastics will not be so conducive to retaining human scents.

Most, if not all, materials have some odour of their own and some are strong enough to be apparent to the human sense of smell. Leather is a good example of a smell that humans can identify and yet a dog can discriminate between human scents on different pieces of leather.

SCENT LIFE

Scent life and thereby the strength of a scent or odour at any particular time is dependent, to a great extent, on the moisture in the atmosphere. The ambient temperature and wind conditions are also important factors.

When dealing with a short time cycle such as the normally accepted periods of time in searching, quartering for a missing person or carrying out a scent discrimination the scent life is a minor factor. In the cases where longer periods of time are involved the scent will disperse according to the prevailing conditions.

Moisture seems to be the basic controlling factor; it would appear that scent cannot be maintained in the atmosphere without it. The ease or difficulty of a dog following a track is dependent on the moisture and the conditions which control the rate of evaporation. The moisture from crushed or bruised vegetation creates a strong odour at the moment the vegetable life is damaged by the tread of a footprint. The result of a dry atmosphere, the heat of the sun and the effect of the wind will be to disperse the moisture and the odour it carries. The drier the atmosphere with supporting conditions the quicker the ground odour and body scent will disperse. A damp cool still day, however, will ensure that scent odours linger on in strength for a considerable period.

A good dog may well find that to follow the movements of a person across a pasture field three hours after the event could be difficult in a very hot drying wind. However, the same movements late at night may be much easier to follow some eight or ten hours later because of the dampness overnight.

As a competitor, tracklayer or a judge, colleagues and I have often discussed and assessed the prevailing tracking conditions, the type of ground and the weather. We have often come to firm conclusions on the probability of achieving a successful track under these conditions, only to find that the dogs know better. Sometimes they prove that the conditions are much better than our assessment and at other times the conditions are apparently much worse.

I recall judging at one trials, on the second day of continuous rain, when the conditions were considered to be extremely bad and yet many dogs completed the track with ease. At another trials on the same ground when I was competing there was a tremendous cloud-burst just after my track had been laid. Half an hour later my dog could not detect any scent at the starting stake. This was the only time this dog failed even to start on a given track. The scent of the tracklayer and the odour from the crushed vegetation had been completely washed away by this deluge of rain.

The police at their National Trials run a hard surface track as one exercise and it is commonly recognized as a lottery. A section of the track is laid on a tarmacadam or concrete road or airfield runway. If a dog works during damp or wet conditions he has a chance but if the surface is dry there is little hope of locating a scent after half an hour.

To illustrate this point I laid an experimental track on the beach one day. The tide was out and I walked alternately along stretches of damp sand just below the high water level and then dry sand above this level. About twenty minutes later the dog was put on to the track and worked the sections on damp sand without any problems but the dry sand conditions proved to be very difficult. This was further proof of the effects of moisture.

We can theorize much about scents and prove some theories, but there is so much we do not know.

7

Tracking

Dogs are used as trackers all over the world and by the various police forces or the armed services. In many instances the dogs are chosen for the sole purpose of tracking. Following the same principle as the gamekeeper breeding from his most natural gundogs they can be the progeny of dogs dedicated to the art of tracking, dogs with the strongest inherited tracking instinct.

Civilians are taking an ever-increasing interest in this field of activity and it is becoming a very satisfying pastime for many people. Although this can be a rather energetic hobby I know of competitors who have discovered its pleasures after reaching retirement age and one well-known and successful competitor decided to call it a day in her eightieth year.

In the UK competitive working trials have tracking as the centre-piece of the various tests, whereas the US and Canadian Kennel Clubs award qualifications for dogs who achieve certain standards in tracking only.

Tracking is probably the most natural use we can make of a dog's olfactory system, his ability to focus on particular scents, to relate one scent or odour to another and to follow the related scents created by a person walking across a piece of ground. Tracking is an instinctive and inherited art; only the dog knows how it is done, only the dog knows which scent or odour is taking his attention and only the dog knows the strength of that scent.

All dogs have this inherited art, but not all of them realize it, nor do they all have the power of concentration nor the scenting sensitivity to make a first-class tracker dog. Any dog will track when he wants, but only on the scents which take his interest and only for as long as he maintains an interest in that particular scent. If a member of the family goes out for a walk just ahead of another and the second party has the dog, one finds invariably that the dog's nose is down at ground level tracking that member of the family ahead of him.

There is no need to teach a dog to track and I believe that we are showing a gross lack of understanding if we try, but we can, however, induce and encourage a dog to use this unique and natural ability. We can create situations where he will gain experience and improve on his ability, but we cannot teach him to track. This does not mean that a sound standard of tracking will be achieved without a great deal of thought, and a good natural tracker can be ruined by the lack of thought or misguided planning. A less strongly motivated dog can easily become a non-starter if insufficient consideration has been given to the task of inducing the correct attitude of mind.

We, as handlers, have much to learn in the art of tracking. We have no inherited instincts to help us, we must learn from our dogs through observation, by watching their reactions and by monitoring their progress. A dog will only track at the request of his human companion if there is sufficient incentive and the best long-term incentive is the sheer joy of tracking plus the pleasure of his handler on completion of the track.

An operational or a competitive dog will normally wear a special harness when tracking with a thirty to forty foot line connecting harness to handler. This helps to ensure that the dog tracks with responsibility and also ensures that the handler is nearby when the dog reaches his objective.

Free tracking, without a harness, can be fun, especially with the family dog. However, this has limited applications unless it is used as a back track, that is having your dog retrace your footsteps to find and return with some lost article such as a dropped glove, the car keys or some such personal possession.

THE TRACK
Wherever a person walks he leaves a trail of body scents and

odours from his clothing. These scents float freely in the atmosphere and will drift and cling to the vegetation as they drop to the ground. There are also odours from shoes and trousers in contact with the ground or vegetation, but most important of all are the odours from bruised or crushed vegetation or even the soil disturbed by each footstep.

On a fresh track most scents and odours will be prominent and the dog will probably focus on the human scent because his incentives are based on this use of body scents. As the time lag between a person walking across a piece of ground and the dog investigating the area increases the airborne scents, those of man and his clothing will diminish and eventually disappear. The ground odours, from shoes or the bruised vegetation, will continue to be emitted into the atmosphere for some considerable time until they too are of little significance.

Fresh tracks will appear to a dog as a continuous scent path and with a wide band of scent he may even track one or two yards on the windward side of the actual footsteps. In time, as the odours become weaker they will only be located in the immediate area of each footprint with a twelve to fifteen inch space between one toe mark and the heel of the next step.

When a person turns to walk in another direction this creates a dead end in that particular direction; the dog will realize that the scent path does not just stop, instinct will tell him to cast around until he locates the change of direction. The scent path from one such turn to another will in future be referred to as a LEG of a track, and each turn will be termed a CORNER.

The start of a track is the area or point where a dog is expected to pick up the scent. On an operational track the point of pick up can be anywhere, the flower bed outside an open window after a burglary, the side of a field where a suspect was spotted from a distance or at the roadside beside an abandoned car. A competitive track will normally start at a definite point and will probably be marked by a post put into the ground for that purpose.

The end of a track is where the dog has reached his objective. With an operational dog this may be at the home of a suspect or at the roadside where the get-away car had been parked. On a competitive track the end will be denoted by the last article dropped on the track by the tracklayer.

A dog is expected to indicate the presence of any article dropped on a track and any such article can be used as evidence against a suspect or can confirm the route taken by a missing child.

THE EVER-CHANGING CONDITIONS

No two tracks are alike, nor do the conditions on a single track remain constant. It may be practical to compare this with a panoramic view as seen by the human eye, where a passing cloud can cause the texture of the hillside to change and the sun, lowering itself in the evening sky, will create a changing sequence of colours or tones so that certain features lose their distinction and others become more clear for a period.

A track changes along its course in accordance with the terrain: the odours from crushed vegetation will alter from one area to another, the edge of a field can be rich in grass or weed vegetation whereas the rest of the field could be newly cut stubble or may even be ploughed. The pasture at the bottom of the field may be very damp and sheltered ensuring good scenting conditions for some hours, yet the top of this field may be open to the wind where the drying atmosphere can shorten the life of the track odours considerably.

The tracklayer may be a missing child, carrying little weight on a pair of small feet, thereby leaving minimal impression on the undergrowth and a short-lived scent, or he could be two hundred pounds of sweating thug in full flight whose heavy boots will leave a very distinctive and long-lasting scenting impression.

Every single footstep on a track differs from the one before it, how else could a dog determine the correct direction of a track? Admittedly on an ageing track the difference must be minute and it is open to debate whether a dog can tell the difference when introduced to these ageing tracks.

I believe that generally dogs can detect the correct direction and may back track some five or ten paces before sizing up the situation then turning to follow in the correct direction.

I did, however, witness one trials with three-hour-cold tracks where the dogs were taken across 'clean' ground at right angles to the track with the choice of going right or left. Every dog was a proven top-class tracker and yet half of them went in the wrong direction. It may have been the conditions on that day, I do not know, but these failures were left unexplained.

Although ground conditions are very important, it is the combination of ground and atmospheric conditions which govern the changing dominance of the various scents or odours on a track. There may well be critical periods in the life of a track when a dog finds it easier to focus on the odour from crushed vegetation rather than the human scent which must be the initial incentive to follow a track, yet the dog must realize that this ground odour is a reliable substitute and will lead him to his objective.

Every track will probably be affected by some sort of interference. This interference may be caused, for example, by sheep, cattle, rabbits or members of the rodent family. I wonder what scent is left by a flock of seagulls which take to the air as a tracklayer approaches, or a flock which land and take rest on top of a newly laid track. To lay a track in a field without knowing that a herd of dairy cattle had been taken in for milking a little earlier could create unsolved and worrying problems because the dog would not settle to his usual steady track.

A dog, especially of the gundog variety, who has had the freedom to chase rabbits or birds at his leisure may well consider it to be his right to leave a track for the more interesting scent of game.

The interference from human cross tracks can create a bigger problem, especially when somebody walks across the ground after the track has been laid, thereby creating a fresher track across the intended line the dog should take.

I have watched a family of four walk straight up the first leg of a track, but if I had not seen them how would I have reacted to my dog's inability to start on an otherwise simple track?

On another occasion I had just finished laying a track and looked round to assess my bearings to find that two youths were walking across the tracking area carrying my marker post from the start of the track.

Tracking interferences are natural hazards and there is a great need to appreciate the existence and significance of such hazards before blaming the dog for failure.

OUR OBJECTIVE

The Dog
Our objective is to create a keen reliable track-sure dog, one who responds to the sight of his tracking harness, who does not require commands to track but patiently waits for the harness to be fitted round his body and as soon as he feels or hears the tracking line being clipped on to the ring, his nose goes down to seek out that track. By means of a build-up in experience and time delays such a dog will eventually be competent to follow a track three hours after it was laid (three hours cold) and of at least half a mile in length.

Ideal conditions can greatly lengthen the workable life of a track and the three-hour period is given as the requirement for the most exacting competition work. To attain a competent and reliable performance under these conditions, however, a dog must be experienced and capable of working out colder and longer tracks.

A dog should be capable of distinguishing between the correct track and cross tracks; cattle or game tracks should not be a problem but the existence of a human cross track can create difficulties and careful conditioning is required to obtain sound results.

Our tracker dog should also be capable of encountering obstacles such as a fence, hedges or walls etc. Did the track-layer negotiate the obstacle or did he walk along beside it? The dog should be prepared to investigate round or across a 'dead' area. A stream will not hold scent and he should be prepared to investigate until the track has been located; on colder tracks a road may cause the same problem. The important point is that the dog should have sufficient enthusiasm to investigate and check out all possibilities.

The Handler

He must learn to understand the principles of tracking and be prepared to accept that the dog knows a great deal more than he does.

He must build up a trust in his dog where each successful track further consolidates the confidence which a handler has in his dog and the dog has in him. The handler must learn to be patient and should accept that he does not know everything about each single track — even if he lays it himself.

Failures will occur which are no fault of the dog. The dog should *never* be blamed for a failure. His skill is a reflection of the handler's knowledge, ability and effort.

Each dog has his limits and so does each handler. Train and practise up to these limits and you can do no better.

MOTIVATION

Tracking requires one hundred per cent concentration from a dog. The best trackers can cut themselves off completely from the outside world whilst they are working and this means fully committed concentration for an unspecified period.

A competitive track will probably take ten to twenty minutes to complete, but a practical track can take a dog across fields, through fences, along ditches and through thickets for two miles or more. If we take a normal walking pace of three miles an hour as our guide there are forty minutes of concentration involved in a track of this nature but many operational dogs are asked to work for longer periods and this requires unstinted dedication.

Consider our own capabilities; how long can we concentrate on a subject without taking a few seconds relaxation? Think of high-speed motorway driving, especially during a busy period, and consider the mental and, at times, physical exhaustion caused by a lengthy spell of fully committed concentration just to stay on the road.

This sort of concentration cannot be achieved without motivation. A dog must have a burning desire to track; he must experience a great sense of enjoyment and satisfaction. At one time hunger gave him the motivation. Hunger and the kill were the incentives which created the instinct which is inherited in our present-day canine companion. We must, however, use or find the forms of motivation which can build up the degree of concentration required for our final objective. In the long run the inducement to track will be the sheer joy of finding and following the specified scent path.

COMPETITION REQUIREMENTS
Competitive tracking in the UK is part of the working trials schedule and there are three different competitive stages which affect the age of track, although the length of track is a common factor at all levels of competition.

The objective is to locate the scent of the tracklayer at the post which marks the start, to follow this track with the greatest accuracy and to indicate the articles left on the track by the tracklayer.

Full details of the tracking requirements are given in Appendix 1, but a brief summary is given here:

Utililty Dog (U.D.) Stake The initial direction of the track is indicated by a second post which is placed about twenty paces from the start. The track will be approximately half an hour cold and half a mile in length. An article will be placed at this half-mile distance to indicate the end of the track. Although the marks for finding the article can be valuable it is not a requirement for a qualification.

Working Dog (W.D.) and Police Dog (P.D.) Stakes One post is used to indicate the start of the track with no assistance being given to locate the direction of the first leg. The track will be approximately one and a half hours cold and half a mile in length. Two articles will be placed on the track with the second indicating the finish. At least one article must be recovered to qualify.

Tracker Dog (T.D.) Stake Again one post is used to indicate the start of the track with no assistance being given to locate the direction of the first leg. The track will be approximately three hours cold and half a mile in length. Three articles will be evenly spaced along the track with the third indicating the finish. Two articles must be recovered to qualify.

The judge has full discretion in the design of his track and will probably include anything from four to fifteen corners. Although the distance between each corner (the legs) is normally walked in a reasonably straight line the judge may well decide to include a curve.

Normal competition track articles can vary tremendously in both size and composition. They can be as small as a golf tee or as large as a shoe, although the size of a matchbox may be more appropriate.

The article may be symmetrical and specially cut for the purpose or may be of an odd shape which could appear to be litter, such as a used shot-gun cartridge, an empty cigarette packet or a crumpled page from a book. Examples of typical articles are shown in Figure 10 (see page 94).

In the United States and Canada, tracking is an exercise on its own where dogs do not normally compete against each other and the only objective is to gain a tracking title. A T.D. (Tracker Dog) title is available in both the United States and Canada where the track can be between half an hour and two hours cold. The length of the track is between 440 yards and 500 yards with a dark coloured glove or wallet at the end of the track and which has to be identified by the dog.

Canada goes a stage further with a more complicated track for the T.D.X. title. This is probably the most advanced stage in competitive tracking within the English-speaking countries. The track is a minimum of three hours cold, at least 1000 yards in length and will probably traverse fences, hedges or the like and will cross at least one road. A fresh cross track is also introduced as an additional hazard.

One further tracking event which is restricted to the police and is part of the schedule for the National Police Dog Trials (UK) is the hard surface track. This is approximately half a mile in length and half an hour cold. The track length has to be laid on a hard surface such as a road or a path without vegetation.

EQUIPMENT FOR TRACKING
Very little equipment is required for tracking but the most important and costly is the harness. Controlled tracking can be carried out best with a properly constructed harness which has been designed for comfort and freedom of head and neck movement so that a dog can take the strain of a tight tracking line through the harness shoulder straps whilst his nose is right down at ground level.

My very first tracking harness was made out of our younger daughter's pram harness; it was very effective and well used until my father bought me a purpose-made leather harness when I qualified my first dog to the level of U.D.Ex.

Although harnesses made from canvas or nylon webbing can be obtained, one made from good quality bridle leather is far superior and worth buying when one considers the hours of pleasure obtained from this chosen pastime. A good well-preserved leather harness will outlast a number of dogs and may well outlast the handler also.

A harness made from canvas webbing can be quite satisfactory but will have a much shorter life and although a nylon harness will certainly last for many years there is always a tendency for the straps to slip and cause discomfort due to the resultant poor fit round the dog's body whilst he is tracking.

Figure 2 shows a sketch for a harness dimensioned to suit a larger dog, say a German Shepherd, with ample adjustment to cover other breeds in a similar size range. The measurements in brackets are suited to a harness for a Border Collie size dog. Any good saddler will make a harness to your requirements.

The connecting link between a tracker dog and his handler is the tracking line. This line should be approximately thirty-six feet in length and it should have a dog lead type of clip at one end for attachment to the harness and preferably a loop at the other end for holding. The most suitable lines for the medium to larger dogs can be obtained from any

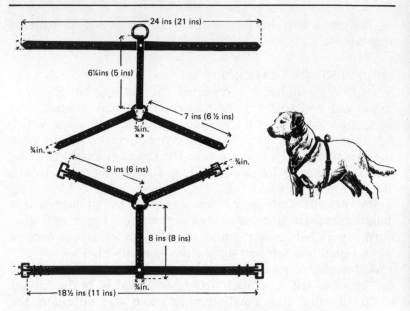

Fig. 2 Tracking harness of a suitable size for larger breeds; for smaller breeds the harness can be adjusted to the measurements shown in brackets.

hardware shop. A good quality cotton clothes rope or waxed cotton window sash cord is ideal. Polypropylene or nylon ropes of similar weight are also suitable but are more likely to cause rope burns on your hands if you have an enthusiastic tracking dog. With smaller dogs a lighter nylon line would probably be more suitable.

A canvas webbing tracking line can be very compact when rolled up with no possibilities of tangles when preparing to track. However, there can be excessive flapping of the line on a windy day and this may well distract a more sensitive dog.

Proper marking posts are not essential and a garden cane may be sufficient to mark the start of a track. However, a good pointed post can prevent a fair amount of frustration when trying to push it into dry, hard ground. Many people find a broom shaft with a nail in the bottom to be a useful piece of equipment.

Two such posts are advisable to accustom the dog to

Fig. 3 Tracking or search post made
from broom shaft or handle about
4 feet long.

competitive conditions and the following instructions can be
helpful for making suitable posts (see Figure 3):

1. Procure a broom or brush shaft about four feet in
   length.
2. Insert the bottom of the shaft into a tight fitting
   metal ring, a ring about one inch in length will be
   sufficient. Alternatively wind wire strands round the
   bottom. This will prevent the wooden shaft from
   splitting.
3. Obtain a five or six inch nail and cut off the head.
4. Drill a hole up the centre of the shaft for a distance
   which will ensure that three inches of the nail will
   remain visible after it has been hammered into this
   hole. When drilling the hole make sure the size is
   slightly smaller than the diameter of the nail to
   ensure a good grip on the wooden shaft.

Articles to find are another necessity, to provide the real
incentive to track. In the early stages they should be of a
good size: a glove, a ball, a 'doggy' toy or a slipper, these can
make ideal articles to start with; later on, items similar to
competition requirements should be at hand. Articles will be
discussed in greater detail at the appropriate stage (see page
90).

ASSESSING YOUR APPROACH TO TRACKING
As mentioned earlier in the text we cannot teach a dog
to track. He already has an inborn instinct; the art is

there but he is unlikely to have the skill or the incentive to use it to suit our requirements until his instinct has been fully cultivated.

Our objective is to condition the dog in such a manner that he will know, without commands, when and where he is expected to locate a track: he is not being asked or told, but is being released and is being given permission to track. The sight of the tracking harness should be sufficient to excite the dog and his expression should be one of expectancy and joy.

Progress may well be slow, but full of promise and pleasure. Even with a good natural beginner and a handler who knows the ropes the progress will be controlled at a pace which will ensure that each step is firmly instilled in the dog's mind.

The natural tracking desire varies considerably from dog to dog. Some are so keen that it is uncanny to see how they can progress so far beyond their handler's capability to understand the complexity of the task at hand, and it is often the handler's short-comings which ruin a good dog. Other dogs are much less motivated and may require a fair amount of inducement before they discover that their olfactory system is much more effective and efficient than their eyes.

Dogs who have had strict obedience instilled into their system may find it difficult to acquire the independence required for tracking and may well find that their obedience-orientated handler is less capable of appreciating the completely different approach required for this form of work. The obedience enthusiast must be prepared to start thinking afresh, discard his obedience training, and return to the status of a novice.

Although the approach to conditioning all dogs for tracking may be similar the purpose for one dog may be quite different from another.

The natural tracker can be built up to a high degree of efficiency without the introduction of articles on a track; he will probably consider any such articles as a hindrance and is likely to ignore their presence. The objective with a dog like this is to influence him, from the beginning, to stop for an article. He requires no inducement to track but he does require an inducement to stop for articles.

At the other end of the scale we have the dog without any interest in tracking; we could call him the less-motivated tracking dog. He requires a strong inducement to enlist nature's gift to achieve *his* objective.

It is important to know whether a dog is a 'natural' or not, as this affects the handler's outlook and his ability to control the progress of training to achieve the prime objectives. To determine a dog's natural response a very simple unsophisticated test can be applied. Whilst out for a walk with your dog go into a field or a park at a time when there are absolutely no distractions and use a piece of ground on which you have not already walked during your present visit to the area. Tie your dog up to a fence post or other suitable object; do not tell him to stay or inhibit him in any way, but just leave him and walk out some fifty paces and then return down wind in a semi-circle as in Figure 4. Whilst you are doing this your dog may jump around and bark; just let him. Do not shout or scold him as you may find that his excitement is a good indication of his desire to sniff out your scent path.

When you return to your dog, untie him and repeat the walk with him on the lead. If he is a 'natural' he will be curious to know where you have been and he will put his nose to the ground to follow your scent path. Your dog may show interest only for twenty or thirty yards or he may track you right round to your starting point. The extent of his interest is dependent on the strength of his inherited instinct. A dog who has been trained to walk on a loose lead at all

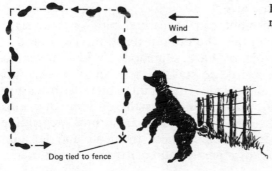

Fig. 4 Determining the natural tracker.

Wind

Dog tied to fence

times, however, may well be too inhibited by the lead to show a natural response. With a dog so conditioned to the lead a truer picture will be obtained by letting him go free to see what reaction comes naturally.

Many dogs will not show any interest in the scent path and may well be saying, 'I do not need to follow that scent to find him, he is on the other end of the lead.' These dogs may have very little tracking ability in their inheritance and some may not have the ability to concentrate for long enough periods, yet others can have a strong tracking instinct lying dormant, waiting for somebody with the correct understanding to bring this potential to the fore.

INDUCEMENTS FOR THE LESS-MOTIVATED DOG

A dog who retrieves or loves to run out for a thrown toy, even if he does not return with it, has a distinct advantage: he has a strong possessive trait and as previously described with the retrieve matrix we are dependent on using or cultivating that possessive trait. The submissive trait is not important, it may even be an inhibiting factor, but we do wish to capitalize on this possessiveness to achieve our objective.

There is no single approach to cultivate possessiveness, although the basic principle of fun and games should be foremost in a handler's mind. Each handler should observe his dog or puppy. Is there a favourite toy? Will food have to be used as an inducement? Would the help of an assistant be an advantage? I can give a few ideas on cultivating this possessiveness, but it is up to the handler to use a specific idea or to develop his own.

The initial inducement can be carried out by using sight instead of scent to obtain the desired reaction. Tie your dog to something suitable or have somebody hold him on his lead. He must not be told to stay or to be quiet as he must not be inhibited in any way. Tease him a little with his toy then walk out and place it in full sight of your dog; this may be five, ten or even twenty paces from him, depending on your dog. Return to him, take the lead and let him take you out to his toy, then let him off the lead for fun and

games with his prized possession. The secret at this early
stage is to have him desperate to go out and claim his own
toy. This can be anything which takes his fancy and if you
are fortunate you may have a variety of such toys which are
equally valuable to him.

Some dogs like squeaky rubber or plastic toys, with others
a rubber bone or ball may take their fancy. One dog I know
of could only be excited with a ball in the toe of a nylon
stocking.

My own German Shepherd bitch, Jeza, was a real country
girl who did not know family life until she was six months
old. She did not know what toys were for and nothing
excited her sufficiently to induce an enjoyable game until I
used a hardboard disc about six inches in diameter. With a
back-hand flip I could make that disc float through the air
like a bird in flight; that was enough for my little country
lass, she would go out like a shot to make the 'kill'. I had a
plentiful supply of discs at that time and certainly needed
them, not only for Jeza but also for friends who realized
what an inducement they could be.

When the sight of the disc was sufficient to stimulate
natural excitement I would walk out about twenty yards
and place it on the grass, return to Jeza and let her take me
out to it on the end of her lead. I would then release her,
pick up the disc and throw it for her. These discs became
her incentive to track.

Young Caro, another German Shepherd, joined our household at the age of fifteen weeks. He was a character and, like
his father, was a natural carrier. By the time he was five
months old he was picking up any piece of wood he could
carry and although he was not retrieving, he was carrying
articles of his own choice. At that time we had a favourite
walk through a country park where timber operations gave
young Caro a tremendous selection of tree cuttings.

After Caro had selected his article for the day and had run
around with it, also teasing Jeza into chasing him with his
piece of wood, this piece of wood became his valued possession. That was the time to tie Jeza up and have Irene, my
wife, hold Caro on the lead whilst I took his piece of wood

and walked into the wind for some thirty paces or so and let Caro see me drop it. I then returned by exactly the same route, took the lead, then let Caro take me at top speed to get his stick. The stick was then thrown for him and he was again in possession of his precious piece of wood. Half a dozen such outings with increasing distance each time had Caro doing one hundred yards before I thought of introducing him to the tracking harness.

Although I had labelled Caro as a less-motivated tracker after applying my usual test, he responded magnificently to the correct inducement for him. Many dogs take much longer and it is a case of progressing at the rate which suits the particular dog.

Another approach which was used to develop Caro's enthusiasm, and is used extensively, with variations, by police dog handlers, is also a basis for manwork training. A piece of leather, canvas, sacking or some such material is ideal for having a tug-of-war with a dog. The excitement of such a game can be a very strong incentive to track for the article. It must be said, at this stage, that personal aggression is not necessary and it is not advisable to mix full manwork training with tracking.

When the dog has accepted this exciting game, short tracks can be laid in the same manner as with Caro and his piece of wood or Jeza and her disc, but in this instance the dog is given full satisfaction with a tug-of-war after finding his article.

A novel variation to this tug-of-war is an old trick which suits a dog who enjoys pulling at the exposed roots of a tree. Hammer a wooden peg into the ground so that the dog can enjoy pulling it out. I have never used this form of incentive but I believe it can be very effective with some dogs.

Unfortunately, there are some dogs without any interest in fun and they are usually dogs who have been brought up in a humourless home or in a breeding kennel where the breeder or his staff have not had the interest or time to help develop the characters of their stock. Some youngsters come through this environment full of character in spite of their lack of stimulus, whilst others lack that spark of life so essential to a tracking dog. This spark, however, may be cultivated with help from another member of the family and food used as the inducement.

Dogs who lack character, either through environment or breeding, often compensate by their excessive loyalty to the family or very close friends. Capitalizing on this factor and the use of hunger can help to stimulate a dog with no real interest in other aspects of life.

Have a member of the family or a favourite friend take the dog's meal for the day and at the usual feeding time. He should walk out some twenty or thirty yards whilst you hold the dog on the lead. The assistant can then call your dog and you should follow at the end of the lead giving every encouragement. On reaching the assistant your dog should be given excited praise by both of you and also be given his food. With the assistant in full view, this procedure need only be repeated until your dog makes an excited and immediate response to the call. In fact it is more encouraging if you have to restrain him physically.

Now choose an area where your assistant can walk out into the wind and drop out of sight some thirty yards away. As soon as your assistant is out of sight, have him call your dog. If you think it is necessary, follow your dog to the hiding place. Excited praise and being given his food is the reward for finding your assistant.

When it has become evident that food is the principal attraction, your assistant is of less importance. The next stage is to make use of a following wind and repeat the process, but this time your assistant removes his jacket, jerkin or some other suitable article of clothing, lays it on the ground and puts the dog's dish of food on top of it. The assistant walks on for a further fifteen yards or so and again drops out of sight. You then allow the dog to run out at the end of the lead. He will probably start off by visually focusing on the spot where your assistant disappeared but will soon realize that his nose is much more dependable and will track the rest of the way to your assistant's jacket and the food. Make sure your assistant keeps out of sight until you have praised your dog and he has finished his food. It is important that you make use of a following wind (see Figure 5), so that the dog does not scent your assistant lying on the ground.

When this stage has been well established and food is the real incentive, your assistant can now be dispensed with. You can tie your dog up and lay your short tracks into the wind with the food in a sealed container, such as a Tupperware box, which has been wiped down to minimize the scent of food. Now it is the knowledge that he will be fed on reaching his objective rather than the scent of it which induces him to track his way out to a meal.

The foundation conditioning which will be described can be applied where the container of food is left with a well-scented article. At a later stage the food can be carried by the handler and be given immediately the dog finds his article.

These are just a few examples of the inducements which can be used to interest a dog into using his nose in a manner which suits our purpose.

A FOUNDATION FOR TRACKING

Each stage of conditioning a dog to track must blend with the previous and the following stages. There are practices to be encouraged at certain stages which are considered to be decidedly harmful at others. Some trainers will have thrown up their hands in horror at a few of my comments in the previous pages, but I hope that the following notes will dispel any apprehension.

I have given details which involve double tracking, i.e. walking straight out then back along the same line, thereby creating tracks in opposite directions and superimposed on each other. When one considers that the alternative involves

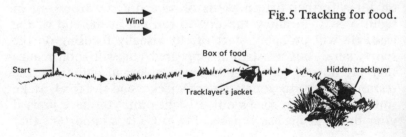

Fig.5 Tracking for food.

Wind

Start

Box of food

Tracklayer's jacket

Hidden tracklayer

walking round in a box or circle to create a single track the dog may well be distracted from the objective by having a choice and he may back track round to the article. In the earlier stages it is also imperative that the time factor between dropping the article and allowing the dog to go out after it be kept to a minimum. Although this practice is decidedly helpful in the early stages it must be stopped as soon as possible to ensure that a forward tracking attitude is developed.

It is also believed by some trainers that the introduction to tracking must be made with the correct equipment, i.e. a tracking harness and line. Many good dogs have been introduced from the start without a harness and I have found it easier to maintain a fun-and-games approach without the formality of a harness and only introduce the use of this equipment when the dog is capable of concentrating for a sixty- to one-hundred-yard track. Also I believe that in Germany, the home of present-day tracking, some top-class dogs are tracking whilst attached to an ordinary collar and a line.

A number of authoritative voices say that a handler should not lay any tracks for his own dog, even in the earliest stages. At the same time I know of a few top-class handlers in the past who would *never* allow any other person to lay commissioning tracks for them. In laying all their own tracks they turned out good, practical working police dogs or competition dogs of some note. This subject will be discussed in greater detail at a later stage.

Although the natural tracker does not require the inducements of the less-motivated dog he must realize that the purpose of the exercise is to find the articles on the track. If the reader has skipped over the earlier details on inducements for the less-motivated dog because he has a 'natural', he would be well advised to go back and read again so that he can co-ordinate the natural desire to track with the need to find articles.

The natural tracker can always be a problem to his handler if he is not induced, from the beginning, to stop for the articles. Even the less-motivated dog who has been properly induced to go out for his article will eventually enjoy his tracking so much that he can, at a later stage, ignore articles because they interrupt the enjoyment of tracking. He can become a 'natural' and the handler will have to ensure that there is always sufficient inducement to stop until it becomes second nature for the dog to become rooted to the spot as soon as he has located an article.

The procedure is now identical for both the natural and the less-motivated dogs, but the purposes differ greatly. The 'natural' is induced to stop at the article and the 'less-motivated' is induced to go out for the article.

The first tracks should be of a length to suit your dog — they may be ten yards or they may be fifty — but it is important that the working of each track be carried out by the dog without any break in concentration. His mind must be fixed on his objective from start to finish. Keenness at the end of a track is as important as keenness at the beginning.

With these initial tracks the dog will normally be on the lead, but make sure that a slip chain, if used, is not on the choke. It may even be desirable to use a leather collar. Dogs who are inhibited by a lead and slip chain may well perform better if released to track free during the foundation stages.

A nice, quiet field away from all distractions is the ideal setting for your foundation work. Position yourself so that you lay your tracks into the wind. Tracking into the wind serves the useful purpose of helping the less-motivated dog to locate his article quickly as he will probably wind it before he goes the full distance. This success encourages longer periods of concentration and therefore more successes. Also, tracking into the wind with the article at the end ensures that no scent has travelled beyond that article, so there is no inducement for the natural tracker to go beyond that point.

To lay those foundation tracks, first tie your dog to a post or let somebody hold him; let him know you have his fun article and walk out the required distance. Let the dog see you place his article but ensure that it is suitably hidden from view until he is almost on top of it. We now wish to avoid the dog catching sight of the article so that achievement through scenting will increase his confidence. Return to your dog by the same route as in Figure 6a, then encourage him to go out as you follow at the end of the lead. The scent of his article will reach him before he has gone the full distance and he should 'home' in on it. He may start off by using his eyes, having seen you walk out, but his nose will soon take control and prove to be much more reliable.

Whenever your dog reaches the article make the most of it. Give him plenty of praise with fun and games, titbits, if you wish, a fun retrieve or a tug-of-war, anything so long as your dog finds tremendous pleasure from stopping at the article.

The next stage is to try carrying out this foundation work with a following wind as in Figure 6b. Although the track does not go beyond the article the wind will certainly carry the scent on for some distance. Your dog may well overshoot the article by a yard or so before realizing it is there but he should turn back to indicate its presence. If he carries on much further without a positive indication of the article he is not ready to progress and more tracks into the wind are necessary.

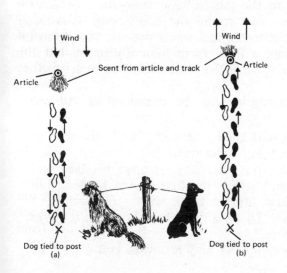

Fig. 6 A foundation for tracking.

DEVELOPING A ROUTINE

Your dog should always know when he is expected to track. The sight of the harness, your own actions and the routine you develop should be sufficient to let him know he is being allowed to track. The only verbal support he should require is a few words of encouragement as he puts his nose to the ground to locate the scent. His reactions, however, can only meet your requirements if you plan each stage and develop the routine gradually so that one stage is in harmony with the next.

The tracking harness is the key; the dog should automatically seek out the track when the harness is fitted and then realize that the job is finished when the harness is removed. To have a dog wandering around with the harness on before he is being asked to track will take away this key to motivation. To leave the harness on the dog after the completion of the track will have the same effect. Some trainers advocate that the dog should become accustomed to the harness before he is given his first track. This may well work with good dogs and well disciplined handlers, but it tends to introduce a sloppy approach and thereby to negate a very natural form of motivation.

The complete development of this routine is based on full canine dedication to the job in hand from the moment the tracking harness is fitted round the dog's body. It is recognized that the initial tracks in harness may be strange to the dog and can detract a little from his enthusiasm, but this should not be a problem if the foundation has been properly carried out.

The final tracking routine can be described as follows:

1. Take your dog with the harness and line to the start of the track, or within five yards of it.
2. Put the harness on your dog, remove his lead and check chain and attach the line to the harness. Immediately release him to track with a few words of encouragement. 'That's a good boy, where is it?' is as good as anything.
3. On finding an article he may return to you with it, he

may stand over it, or he may lie down beside it. These are only some of the options, but on finding the last article or on recognizing that you are lost you remove the harness immediately to let your dog know that he is not required to track any further.

We can bend a few of our rules in the early stages to build up the connections, so long as we do not forget our final objective. At this stage, the foundation has been developed, your dog has great enthusiasm for his article and he recognizes that his nose is an ideal tool to locate the scent path and the article.

The harness can now be fitted round the dog immediately prior to laying another foundation track: straight out, drop the article and straight back. In the meantime your dog is tied to a post with his lead — a benching chain and leather collar is a good alternative — or he is held by a friend. Return to your dog, clip your lead to his harness and let him go out ahead of you to track down his article. The harness may distract him a little but give him an abundance of encouragement and follow at his speed. On reaching the article give him a few seconds of fun, remove the harness then give him much more fun.

If you lay the track before fitting the harness at this stage of his education he may well lose some or all of his enthusiasm to track. You wish to have his mind firmly fixed on the track from the second you leave him to lay it. On finding the last article, your enthusiasm with fun and games is again keeping his mind on the objective whilst the harness is still attached. At this early stage removing the harness immediately he finds the article can inhibit him at the moment he requires praise for successfully completing his assignment. The use of his lead instead of the tracking line has the purpose of maintaining the close contact of foundation tracking. If the full length of a long line is used he may well wonder why you are so far back and this experience plus the new feeling of a tracking harness could well be too great a distraction.

Tracks can now be developed as a single scent path, as in

Figure 7, where the first leg only is used for tracking and finishing at the article. This first leg should be laid into the wind so that article finding is easy and positive. After dropping the article the tracklayer should carry on walking for some ten to fifteen paces then return at some distance from, but parallel to the working leg of the track to ensure that the track is not contaminated by the return. The tracking line can now be used and the applied length be extended as confidence is gained.

One or two tracks in a session are quite sufficient and if you are laying a second immediately after working the first remember to remove the harness for the short period and use a clean piece of ground well clear of your first track.

Although enthusiasm must be considered to be of top priority, the fitting of the harness prior to laying a track should be stopped as soon as possible, but not at the expense of lost enthusiasm to start a track.

The importance of a short time lag between laying and working the track can be vital. The time taken in preparing harness and line etc. after a track has been laid can be critical if we wish to maintain the maximum of enthusiasm.

When you feel that the harness does not need to be fitted

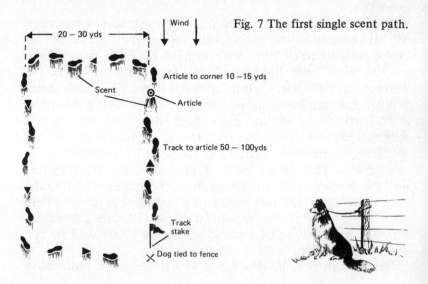

Wind

Fig. 7 The first single scent path.

20 – 30 yds

Article to corner 10 –15 yds

Scent

Article

Track to article 50 — 100yds

Track stake

Dog tied to fence

before the track has been laid, prepare the harness and line by having them laid out all ready before laying the track and make sure that the line is free from tangles or knots. When you have laid the track your dog should be impatient to start; do not disappoint him by taking too long to prepare him. Hamfisted or fussy handling at this stage can be the biggest cause of dogs going off the boil, and then handlers wonder why their dogs have lost enthusiasm.

When single leg tracks of one hundred yards or so are being worked, a change to tracks with a following wind can be laid to give the dog experience of realizing that an article can be present without prior warning. Cross wind tracks can also be added to his repertoire. On these very fresh tracks with a cross wind he may well track some three to six feet on the windward side of the track and on occasions may track wider, come back on the track and then work wide again. Do not worry about this lack of accuracy because he will work much closer to the scent source as he becomes more experienced and the tracks are colder.

A corner can now be included in the track, but again the first leg should be walked into the wind to ensure that no scent has drifted beyond the corner (see Figure 8a). A first leg of some hundred or one hundred and fifty yards will give the dog a chance to settle in before reaching the corner, he will then cast round until he finds the new direction. This is where the importance of enthusiasm becomes evident.

An enthusiastic dog will be very annoyed at losing the track and will busy himself to relocate it. He will probably learn the first lesson of finding a 'lost' track. However, a dog who is lacking in enthusiasm is likely to flounder at this first minor obstacle and will probably require a great deal of encouragement and help to continue round the first corner. This kind of situation is a bad omen for the future and the handler must realize that he is on a 'loser' unless he goes back and achieves a greater response to the initial inducement.

With the article placed some twenty to twenty-five yards beyond the corner the effect of any slight wind change will not be sufficient to carry the scent on to the first leg. This could induce the dog to cross over and miss out on part of

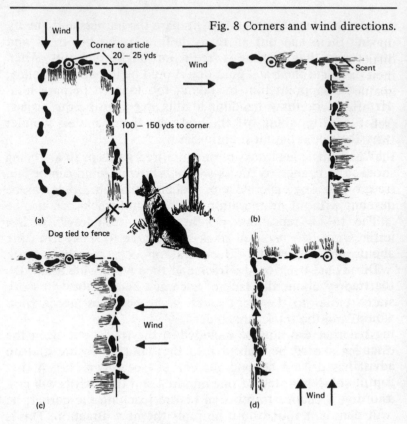

Fig. 8 Corners and wind directions.

Wind

Corner to article
20 – 25 yds

Wind

Scent

100 – 150 yds to corner

Dog tied to fence

(a)

(b)

Wind

Wind

(c)

(d)

the track. This distance also ensures that a full cast does not take the dog beyond the article so that he misses it. To find his article some twenty yards or so after taking his first corner will give the dog great confidence in his own ability to think out a problem and meet with success, i.e. finding his favourite toy. Remember a handler's confidence can only be a product of his dog's success.

Corners involving cross winds should now be laid and it could be advisable to lay the first few with the second leg going into the wind, as in Figure 8b. This gives your dog a choice of direction as the scent from the second leg will be carried beyond the corner. This should not cause a problem, but any attempt to go in the wrong direction by a greater distance than the length of the tracking line should be countered by your refusal to move until he recasts and picks up on the correct direction. A continuation of this type of difficulty will necessitate corners at a slight angle which is increased with every track so that the change in direction is gradually introduced.

Corners which create a following wind with the second leg (see Figure 8c) should not cause any problems. So long as the dog has the enthusiasm to cast there will be scent in only the one direction. Guaranteed success with cross winds should make corners with a following wind on the first leg (see Figure 8d) a simple conclusion to another stage of development.

The article can now be placed further from the corner until each of the two legs on the track has been lengthened to about one hundred and fifty yards.

During this period of development the dog has watched the tracks being laid and there has not been any need to use a starting post to indicate the start of the track, although there would have been no harm in using one. As competitive tracking necessitates a post at the start of the track and it is essential to know exactly where the track can be located, it is advisable to introduce and use a starting post until the full routine has been developed. The post can then be considered as optional if other natural markers are available.

A time delay of a few minutes between laying the track and preparing to work it can now be introduced and this will have one of two possible effects.

1. A more enthusiastic dog because he is annoyed at being kept waiting.
2. A relatively uninterested dog because waiting has dampened his enthusiasm. He is no longer motivated and is just not ready to progress.

The time lag can be extended to some ten minutes or so, the track length can be increased gradually to about four hundred yards and two or three corners be introduced to create a build-up of experience whilst developing the routine.

Again the dog can be tied to a post so that he can watch the track being laid or it may be more convenient to leave him in the car if it can be positioned so that he can watch the start of the track being laid.

During this period a routine has been established where the dog knows that the presence of his harness means tracking and your soft words of encouragement whilst fitting the harness will have helped to reinforce the routine. Unsighted tracks can now be introduced and this is a very important stage of development. It is the stage which proves the value of a sound foundation followed by the development of the tracking routine in the dog's mind.

Your dog can now be left out of sight whilst you lay the track. Leave him in the car or in somebody's care, but as soon as you have laid the track take him to the starting post and prepare him in the normal manner.

Distance and the age of the track can now be gradually extended to the full half-mile in length and half an hour cold. Additional corners will have to be included — four to six should be sufficient with most of them at right angles. An obtuse-angled corner should not create any problems but an acute-angled corner can encourage a dog to cross from one leg to another and it may be advisable to study the effects of wind before adding acute corners to his repertoire. The distance between each corner can also be varied and track legs can vary between fifty and three hundred yards. There is little value in making a track leg any longer and shorter legs at this stage may well cause confusion with some dogs.

TRACKING PROGRESS

Enthusiasm for tracking is much more important than working long tracks or extended time delays. Each dog progresses at his own pace and achievements can only be assessed by determining the canine enthusiasm in conjunction with the length and age of the tracks. The last fifty yards of a track are just as important as the first fifty. If the dog's enthusiasm diminishes before he reaches the article at the end of the track it is too long, too old or a combination of both.

The amount of concentration a dog can give is not limitless. It takes time to build up the amount of concentration which will finally be required. Every break in that concentration whilst tracking must be a cause for concern.

A programme for any form of canine training must be flexible and a tracking programme is no exception. There are, however, a few guide lines which should be considered when planning your future work load:

1. Each stage from the initial foundation right through to the full competitive practical requirements should allow for the need to consolidate before progressing from one stage to the next. A qualification through one competitive stage does not necessarily mean that the dog is ready to progress to the next.

2. Although puppies can be introduced to tracking and benefit greatly from this form of activity, it must be remembered that their ability to concentrate should be related to their stage of maturity. I believe also that the sensitivity of the olfactory system is related to maturity and it is safe to assume that mental and olfactory maturity is closely related to the dog's age. Any programme of progression involving young dogs must take any lack of maturity into consideration.

3. Some dogs thrive on tracking and can be given a track every day for a lengthy period before they become bored with a once enjoyable outlet for their enthusiasm. I wonder how many young brides have mistakenly served up their loved one's favourite dish every day in an attempt to make him happy! Even a dog can get too much of a good thing!

The police can take a new dog and a raw handler and have them comfortably working a full half-mile, half-hour-old track by the end of a three-month general training course, but other dogs will be discarded in the process because they will not make the grade in a reasonable time.

I find myself averaging two tracks per week during the first eighteen months to two years of my dog's working life. Starting at the age of four to six months the youngsters are given plenty of time to develop. Sometimes we manage as many as four tracks during one week, whilst for other periods

Fig. 9 A tracking record.

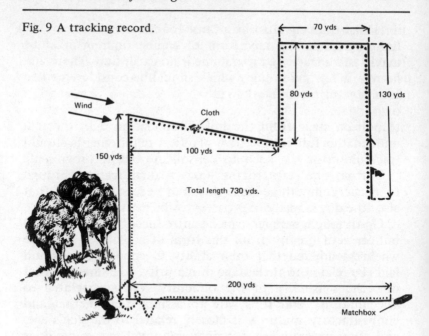

LOCATION – Bathgate hills, cattle grazing field. Sunday 11th June. Laid: 7.30 a.m. Worked: 8.30 a.m. (1 hour old). Laid by: self. Two articles. Moderate wind.
COMMENTS – very keenly and nicely worked until last corner (hillock with trees). There appeared to be some sort of interference, probably early morning game or cattle. Help required to get clear of the area. Completed the last leg without problems. Found both articles.

of a few weeks at a time we may not track at all. I do not believe we have hindered our progress either way.

    4.   A tracking record giving a history of progress is more important than formulating a precisely timed programme for the future. It is the history of progress which controls your attention to the future. Figure 9 shows an entry from my tracking record book.

HANDLING TECHNIQUES
Although the foundation and routine development sections have concentrated on creating the sound basis of a tracking dog, this work can be jeopardized by inexperienced or inconsiderate handling.

Handlers must always remember that they are the weak link in a tracking partnership. If you are fortunate your dog may well be able to carry your deficiencies for a period but he will finally be brought down to your level of competence. It is up to the handler to learn as much as possible about his own function to ensure that his dog is given every opportunity to perform at his best and the handler must bring his level of understanding nearer to the expertise of his dog when tracking.

The application of handler techniques involves the ability to plan and lay tracks suited to the dog's standard of work, also to apply sensible and sympathetic line control.

Good, thoughtful tracklaying generally goes unnoticed, but can go a long way towards avoiding unnecessary problems when the dog is working the track. Two legs of a track being laid rather close with a cross wind can entice an inexperienced dog away from the correct line. Any uncertainty over selected landmarks when laying the track can cause greater confusion, especially when the dog is considered to be wrong, and this situation can be aggravated still further by inconsiderate line control.

The handler who lays a track for his dog can easily affect his dog's attitude towards tracking if he makes incorrect use of his knowledge of the track. On the other hand he can prevent problems and assist his dog to gain experience by the skilful use of his knowledge combined with sensible line control.

The foundation and development of the tracking routine has been described with the handler laying tracks for his own dog. This is not essential if the assistance of a well-experienced tracker dog handler is available. Such a person can be a vital factor in the development of a future tracking partnership. It must be said, however, that many good, experienced handlers are adamant in their view that a handler should refrain from laying tracks for his own dog. The reasons for this opinion do have some validity and they are:

1. If the handler knows exactly where the track is he is likely to transmit that information through the tracking line to his dog, possibly without realizing it.

2. If a dog is brought up on his own handler's track scent he may not know that he can track on other scents.

At this stage, I will only say that I have yet to meet an experienced handler who has ruined a dog of his own by laying his own tracks. The reasons are probably based on observations of the failures of some inexperienced handlers and the causes of these failures may well have been mis-interpreted. I have now handled six dogs through to tracking qualifications and in each case approximately eighty per cent of the tracks were laid by myself. I have also been involved in helping quite a number of novice handlers as they learned the art of line control whilst they worked their dogs on their own tracks.

There is no doubt that you do need to apply a great deal of self-control whilst handling a dog who is working a track you laid yourself. It is very easy for a handler to communi-cate his own knowledge through the tracking line when he knows exactly where the track goes, instead of encouraging the dog to develop his own tracking technique. A handler can apply a little extra tension on the line and thus inadvertently let his dog know that he is coming to an article or a corner, or indicate the correct direction when his dog is casting at a corner. The sensitivity of the tracking line can tell a dog many things if it has been used as a means of communication from handler to dog.

The attentive handler can learn a great deal by studying his dog at work. How does he react to a corner? Does he normally cast wide? Does he overshoot, and by how much, with a following wind? Does he track parallel with the scent path when there is a cross wind and by how much? With the full detailed knowledge of a track a handler is prepared for a dog's reactions and can study them as they arise. Without that knowledge during the initial learning period a handler can fail to recognize his partner's reactions and possibly fail to co-operate fully with his dog's requirements.

Those handlers who advocate the use of other people as tracklayers for novice dogs will probably agree that this approach is only practical if an experienced handler is available to help. This experience can then be used to control the handler and assist in teaching him to interpret his dog's reactions; this is what is meant by the expression 'learning to read your dog'. Those who have this kind of invaluable assistance available are unlikely, perhaps, to need this book.

The alternative is to use an inexperienced tracklayer and to my mind there is no poorer combination than a novice handler with an inexperienced tracklayer. A novice who cannot find a suitably experienced assistant is strongly advised to 'go it alone'. If I meet up with any tracking problems during my dog's working career I immediately revert to laying all the tracks for the dog myself until the problem has been overcome and we have again consolidated on successful tracks.

Referring to the other problem foreseen by some experienced handlers regarding the change over from the handler's scent to that of a stranger, the reintroduction of a few foundation tracks by an assistant can soon overcome any reluctance to change.

Tracklaying is not such a simple task that anybody can be asked and left to carry out the function. It is well known that there are a few experienced and successful handlers who seem to have little sense of direction. They may be reasonably competent on the end of a tracking line but have difficulty in applying the disciplines of a tracklayer.

I remember one experienced handler who offered to lay tracks at a competition. The judge's track shape was simple and perfectly clear but this tracklayer managed to cross the first leg of the track whilst laying the third. The ground was open and the starting post was quite visible, but he took the post marking the start of another track as his marker. The track was quite useless and resulted in the waste of valuable time and an excellent piece of ground.

Some tracklayers go armed with pencil and paper which is very commendable. They note any landmarks and know precisely where the track has been laid, but back at the starting post it may become apparent that there are two landmarks which appear very similar and far enough apart to cause concern. There are times when a clump of heavy grass or a patch of heather used as an integral marker within the track may be completely out of sight when standing back at the starting post.

To walk a straight line when laying a track is not so easy unless the tracklayer applies a certain amount of self-discipline and also makes use of suitable landmarks. The most helpful approach is to choose an easily identified distant marker, but make sure it cannot be confused with another. Walk straight out towards the marker for the appropriate distance, keeping your eyes fixed on it the whole time. If you take your eyes off the marker for five seconds you will probably find that you have changed direction slightly. At each turn choose another landmark or a point between two suitable markers and continue with your track. It is preferable to use distant markers where possible. To use a tree or bush within the tracking area is acceptable on isolated occasions, but to use them regularly would encourage the dog to cast at every bush or tree in expectation of a corner or an article.

Although distances are usually quoted in yards the number of average paces when walking is a satisfactory substitute. If the distance is quoted in metres an extra pace for every ten metres will accommodate the difference, i.e. 300 metres will require 330 paces.

A tracklayer stopping to drop an article will probably create a small area with a much stronger odour. With both feet relatively close together at that point and probably a slight twisting of the feet, especially if the tracklayer turned to note suitable landmarks, any vegetation will have received very severe crushing compared to the normal footprint. This change in odour strength can give an indication to a dog that there is something of note in the area. The very same effect can result when making a corner on a track. This additional odour strength can be used to help and encourage a young dog to expect an article or a corner. So long as the presence of these strong patches is realized by the handler they can be used to advantage; on the other hand, special care can be taken by the tracklayer to ensure that he continues walking when he drops an article or changes direction.

Top and centre: Author demonstrating the introduction to retrieving with Tanfield Atholl of Ardfern ('Caro'): teaching Caro to hold the index finger and to carry as the handler walks backwards.

Below: A Border Collie indicating and picking out the correct cloth in a Class 'C' scent discrimination exercise at a championship show.

Crest of Muirside, a Border Collie, shows us the Class 'A' scent discrimination routine.

Above left: Handler places the article into the gloved hand of her assistant. The glove is of a loose-fitting industrial type.

Above right: Crest is given scent from the handler's hand.

Left: A neat pick up of the correct article.

Tighorain Muffin Man ('Bry'), a Springer Spaniel, demonstrates the Class 'C' scent discrimination exercise.

Above left: Bry is given the scent via a cloth scented similarly to the correct cloth in the line-up.

Above right: Bry shows purpose of mind as he goes up the line of cloths.

Right: The picture tells its own story — a beautiful presentation before completing the exercise.

Police dog Hausfroeng
Fraser U.D.Ex. during a
tracking training session.
Above: Starting a track.
Note that the line has been
laid out and is free of
snags.
Left: Seeking out a change
in direction of the track.
Below left: Fraser has now
located the change in
direction of the track.

A tracklayer should study the effect of wind on any leg, corner or the positioning of articles. Two legs of a track being rather close with a cross wind can be inadvisable for a young dog working very fresh tracks, but these conditions should not affect a more experienced dog working a much older track. On the older tracks most of the peripheral scents will have dispersed and the close proximity of the other leg would probably go unnoticed or be ignored by the dog.

A corner which is too acute can cause similar problems and the presence of an article can also be a strong inducement to leave one leg of the track and take a short cut across to the more interesting scent on the other leg.

It is important that a tracklayer should remember where the track has been laid, but it is equally important he should recognize that he is not infallible. If a dog seems to be tracking well the tracklayer should consider very deeply before condemning the dog for overshooting a corner or for deviating from a straight leg. We as humans are just as likely to be wrong, but at the same time it can do much harm to allow a dog to deviate far from the scent path he is working. A tracklayer should strike the correct balance and this again illustrates the value of a tracklayer who is also an experienced tracker dog handler.

The control of a tracking line is an art and one which should be developed with the greatest respect for the dog's feelings. Sensitive and considerate line control will be rewarded by a dog who accepts the resonsibility of being a senior partner.

The tracking line should be taut whenever possible with the tension being applied by the dog, the handler maintaining sufficient steady resistance to ensure that the line remains taut. When preparing to track the line should be laid out or thrown out in such a manner that knots or tangles have been avoided, or at least sorted out before the harness is fitted to the dog as connecting the line to the harness is the signal to track. The handler should allow tension to be applied from the start to ensure that the line remains taut and is allowed to run through both hands which are as far apart as possible. When the looped end of the line reaches the hand at the rear it is time for the handler to move forward to ensure that a steady tension is maintained. If this function is carried out properly the dog will not feel any jerk on the line as you follow him on the track.

When the dog stops or casts any loose line should be drawn in and, if necessary, be held up high to allow the dog to pass underneath and so avoid a tangle of line and dog's legs as he casts. Some very enthusiastic dogs can cast at such a speed that there is little time to draw the line in and lift it up high enough. On these occasions it is much simpler to let the line drop to the ground so that the dog can cast right over it. There may be a chance of him getting caught up with the line, but a loose line just below body height would present much more of a problem. If your dog does get tangled in the line, do not blame him. Tell him to stay, go up to him and sort out the problem, give him a few words of praise and encouragement to continue with the track.

Under normal tracking conditions the full length of the line should be used but your arm from elbow to shoulder should be used as part of a shock absorbing unit to help maintain steady tension on the line. During a steady track your arm should not be extended at full length but held with the elbow in line with your body. This allows for the full extension of your arm when it is necessary together with a slight quickening of your feet to maintain the tension on the line and regain the neutral arm position. The presence of any bushes or high undergrowth may necessitate a raised arm position to keep the line clear.

Obstacles such as a ditch, a fence or a wall, should be anticipated. When it looks as if an obstacle will have to be negotiated move in towards your dog to give yourself some free line to work with. I have seen a dog stopped in mid-air when jumping a ditch because the handler did not have line to spare.

A barbed-wire fence can cause its own problems, but it is best to hold the dog firm when he has decided to investigate the other side. Keep the tension on the line as you move towards the dog, let him through the fence to investigate and when he decides that the track continues on the other side hold him verbally if you can whilst you negotiate the fence. A young keen dog may be difficult to stop, however; in this case try to snag the line on a barb until you are successfully over the fence, clear your line then proceed with praise for your dog. A barbed-wire fence is always an inconvenience and only practice will help to minimize any problem.

Although competition regulations only stipulate that a dog should indicate the presence of an article which must be recovered by the handler, it is essential to train a dog to stop at articles. He may pick up the article and return to you with it but it is better if he stays where the article is found. With a dog who is eager to continue tracking it is best to hold him firm, keep the tension on the line and move towards him. On securing the article allow him to proceed and let the line through your hands with a steady tension as you would at the start of the track.

In the early days of tracking I would recommend that the spare line at the start of the track or at any stage during the track be left to drag on the ground. Some experts advocate that any spare line should be coiled and held in your hand. Although I fully agree with this practice it may not be practical with a very enthusiastic dog and it does require much attention to become expert at it. I believe that any attention to detail can be of far greater value if directed to watching your dog for indications. A handler must be alert to his dog's actions when the line is being drawn in or being played out and I do not believe that this is the time to be trying to coil or uncoil a tracking line. When a dog has settled down and is well experienced and if the handler has the time to think about the finer points, coiling any spare line can prevent possible snagging of the end in undergrowth.

The tracking line is a one-way communication system, from the dog to the handler, and this shows up to the greatest advantage when tracking at night. As most practical tracks are carried out during the hours of darkness, the handler of an operational dog knows exactly what his dog is doing by the 'feel' of the tracking line. He cannot see his dog for much of the time but that line of communication tells him all he wants to know. A handler trying to communicate back through the line will find that the messages will become scrambled with the information travelling in the opposite direction and this can only lead to a confused partnership.

Unfortunately many novice handlers treat the tracking line as an extra long lead which they jerk, tug or pull when they are displeased with their dog's performance. No wonder an unintentional jerk stops a dog in his tracks and has him saying 'What have I done wrong this time?' The line could be snagged on a bush, caught round a tree when casting or some other innocent cause, but to the dog it means 'I'm wrong again.' His enthusiasm has had a dent and taken another step towards confused bewilderment. However, a dog who is accustomed to a sensibly controlled tension on the line will accept the occasional snarled line without questioning the cause.

Other handlers, although studious in their approach, are quite unconscious of their line control failings. I knew of one student of the art who was having problems with her dog dashing out full of enthusiasm at the start of the track then casting around at the end of the line with a diminishing inclination to continue. Fortunately observation highlighted the fault. This handler was not fully prepared to move forward as the end of the tracking line came into her hands, and the subsequent jerk before she moved off broke the dog's concentration and ability to settle into the track.

Although I explained the cause of the problem on a number of occasions this handler could not seem to overcome her slow start until I gave her the harness with the line attached and asked her to run out at the speed of her dog as I took control of the line. In the first such experiment I let this handler experience her dog's reaction to the jerk from the line, then I let her experience the smooth take-off as I maintained tension on the line and moved forward before I became an extension of that line. The next lesson was a reversal of roles where I played the part of the dog and our student handler was asked to apply the necessary line control. We went through the same procedure until I could move out at a suitable speed without feeling any appreciable change in tension on the line as she moved to follow. When she started tracking again with her dog she controlled the line beautifully and the problem was resolved.

Another aspect of line control is to ensure that the dog feels his responsibility. A tracking line without sufficient tension can give some dogs the feeling of freedom to dart about or to develop a careless attitude to their task and this may result in grossly overshooting corners or meandering off the track for other interesting odours. The correct amount of tension does ensure that a responsible attitude prevails.

Another student who worked a nice German Shepherd bitch was faced with this careless attitude because of her dog's happy and untroubled disposition. Again with this student she found it difficult to apply tension to the line; she was frightened that she would spoil her dog. In this case the instructor grasped the student's coat and forced her to slow down to a suitable pace whilst he encouraged the dog in his own gentle way. After a few tracks like this the student appreciated the value of a speed controlled to suit her dog and the partnership settled into a purposeful combination.

My own bitch, Jeza, tended to overshoot corners for quite a distance when there was a following wind. A little more tension on the line with a few gentle words of encouragement was sufficient to ensure that she did not take me beyond a corner before casting right round to make contact with the next leg of the track.

It is very important that verbal restraint should never be applied at any time on a track and when extra tension is applied a few words of encouragement will ensure that the dog does not feel obliged to relax. The purpose of tension is to control the pace without reducing the dog's enthusiasm.

Many experienced handlers maintain that a handler should not speak to his dog whilst he is tracking. Basically this is sound advice but should not be considered as a golden rule not to be broken. A good dog can shut out everything irrelevant happening round him whilst he is tracking. If the track is all-important to him, his concentration requires a direct challenge before it can be broken. I have watched rabbits and game birds emerge from under a dog's nose whilst he was tracking without a falter in his step. I have handled a dog who passed within a yard of two Pipe Band drummers at practice and it was the silence, with their astonished look, as we passed them which brought the dog's attention to their presence: he ignored the noise but noted the sudden silence. During another practice track this dog stepped over a very surprised and embarrassed courting couple who had taken refuge in a quiet secluded spot one summer evening.

All these events happened to my first tracking dog, Quest, and at that time I did not appreciate the significance of his powers of concentration and dedication. I did discover, however, that if I tried to instruct him during a track or disturbed his concentration with a reprimand of any sort, he lost interest completely. He would seem to say 'If you know better than me, you can carry on and finish it.'

It is, of course, correct to say that a handler should not nag or natter away at a dog whilst he is tracking but there are times, especially in the earlier stages, when encouragement or praise given quietly can help to give a dog that little bit of extra confidence which can make a difference to the limit of his concentration.

Any factor which breaks the steady pace of a dog whilst tracking requires special attention from the handler. If he stops to investigate, casts round or changes direction the handler should ask himself 'What is the reason? Is he casting at a corner or is there some sort of interference?' If the handler knows the direction of the track he can ask himself if he could have read the situation without that prior know-ledge. How well can he trust his dog to stop at an article? Or how competent is his dog at sorting out the situation in the area of interference?

It is important that a dog should be given the opportunity of investigating until he is satisfied, and it is essential that a positive error on the part of the dog must be countered as soon as possible. Any dog who deviates from a track by more than the length of the tracking line (twelve yards) is heading for trouble and should certainly be corrected before he has increased the distance appreciably. (Competitive tracks are, of course, excluded from this statement.)

There are times when an error has been made and it can be

more damaging to attempt recovery. If the dog has crossed from one leg of a track to another, has indicated the new leg and is intent on taking it, confusion will result from taking him off and going back to the area of his departure from the earlier part of the track. This is a problem for the handler and tracklayer only and should be sorted out without the involvement of the dog.

A sound handling technique can often help to prevent a dog from leaving the track, but there can be occasions when a dog may temporarily lose the scent path. The scent could be very faint in a particular area or there may be some sort of interference. As the dog searches round for the track he can only widen his area of search if you, as the handler, move to give him greater scope and every step you take could be drawing your dog further from the track. You should stand still and give your dog every opportunity to work out the problem. If your dog has overshot the corner his chance of picking up the track is reduced by every yard he has gone beyond the corner and it can be a very useful practice to step back a few paces to give him a better chance of retrieving the situation.

Whilst your dog is exhausting all possibilities note exactly where you are and the route you have just taken, you may even find it helpful to make a heel mark in the ground. These are important points to keep in mind if you have to move in search of the track. It is so easy to wander away from a known spot on the track and fail to relocate it.

As one objective is to achieve a track-sure dog and to take pride in reaching that goal with the minimum of lost tracks the most successful handlers in competitions are the least experienced at relocating those lost tracks. To blunder on to a leg of a track after wandering around lost may give some handlers great satisfaction, but there is no credit due to dog or handler. A track lost, then regained in this manner must be considered as a total failure.

However, no practical tracker-dog handler can accept failure so easily and he must try to assess the region of error in an attempt to retrieve the situation. It is often pure guesswork, intuition or sound reasoning which turns failure into success.

When a track has been lost the handler must put his dog before any personal drive to complete the track and this means a continuous reviewing of the situation until the track has been relocated or the decision has been made to call it a day. To overdo the searching to relocate a track, even with a keen dog, can eventually affect his enthusiasm and also his trust in the handler as a competent partner. To try and force a dog into continuing the track when it has eventually been relocated can have a few undesirable side effects. Some dogs will act as if they were tracking just because it seems to please their master and they can finish up taking a direct route to anywhere, irrespective of the right track. Other dogs will become more confused and will find themselves quite incapable of tracking. Some handlers believe that if they walk round the rest of the track with the tracklayer and the dog in harness that the dog may decide to restart, or when the article is pointed out to him he may realize that he should have tracked round to it. I do not think a dog understands these human thoughts and they may even inhibit future performances. When a track has been lost it is a failure: the sooner a new and easier track is laid and then worked the better.

Punishment or giving vent to one's feelings at the expense of the dog when a track is lost can do nothing but harm and will never induce more satisfactory results on future tracks. I have witnessed this sort of conduct and have seen the continued deterioration of good, natural tracking dogs at the hands of a few unsympathetic and inconsiderate handlers. Although the dog has become the scapegoat for these failures, the handler has also paid a high price for his attitude.

TRACK ARTICLES

The foundation for tracking has been based on the inducement to find articles at the end of the track and so far the items used have been well-known favourites belonging to the dog. They have been well impregnated with the dog's and your own scent; they are fun articles — the reason for tracking.

The introduction of new and strange articles on the track

may initially result in the occasional failure to indicate their presence and it is important that one of the old favourites be placed at the end of the track to ensure a successful conclusion to a nicely worked track. This old favourite is now known as the 'saver' where the finding of it means fun and games and the maintenance of the tracking inducement.

The routine to date has built up the ability and concentration to a half-mile, half-hour-old track. A good-sized, fresh article, probably the size of a glove, with the tracklayer's scent only can now be placed on the ground about ten to fifteen yards before the 'saver' is dropped. The last leg of the track should be laid into the wind to ensure that the dog picks up the scent of the article before he reaches it. By laying these tracks yourself you know exactly where the article is and you can ensure that he does not overshoot the article until he recognizes that there are different articles as well as one of the old favourites on the track. On finding the article he is then encouraged to track the further few yards to get to his 'saver'.

It is very important that your dog learns from the start that he should stop at the fresh, well-scented articles and he may at first require verbal notice of its presence. The dog will know that it is on the track when he reaches it and failure to stop is to ignore its presence. To use a small or poorly scented article at this stage would only create excuses for failure to locate it.

A routine can now be developed to establish the dog's reaction to finding an article. Should he stand over it, lie down beside it, pick it up and stay, or bring it back to you? The choice is yours, but he should not be forced into any of them and if one approach stands out as being natural to the dog, use it.

If you are undecided, the easiest method is to have your dog stand over the article until you go to him for it. This method only requires restraint. When the dog indicates the presence of an article, stop, praise him and hold him at that spot whilst you walk towards him, drawing in the line to maintain tension and prevent him from moving forward. Keep praising your dog, pick up the article and, with encouragement, permit him to continue tracking for the final few yards to the 'saver', his favourite article.

It can be very impressive to watch a dog going into the down position when he finds the article. This, I believe, is the ultimate in control and can be well worth achieving, but not at the expense of canine enthusiasm. The down position is a submissive one and any attempt to apply a demanding attitude will certainly affect a dog's desire to indicate or stop at an article. If the dog can be induced into the down position with the reward of titbits or any other pleasant form of inducement then it can be well worth doing.

The moment a dog has the article in his mouth it becomes dual scented, although probably not as strongly as the well-used 'saver'. It is important, at this early stage, that you get the dog accustomed to articles without his scent; after all it was his scented 'saver' which has induced him to stop and if his new articles become impregnated with his scent he may ignore the single scented ones. The use of cross or following winds on the leg of the track containing the article will soon prove the dog's reaction to the lack of warning that an article is present. No attempt should be made to reduce the size of the articles until he is proficient at finding the larger ones.

To date the incentive to track has been built up on a single article at the end of the track, then the use of a 'saver' just beyond the article. The dog may well be conditioned to relaxing now, knowing that he has finished at this article or just beyond. If an additional item is placed in the middle of the track the dog may not want to go any further. How then do we introduce additional articles? This can be done by gradually increasing the distance between the article and the 'saver' until the article is about half-way along the track. Another article can then be placed just prior to dropping the 'saver' and if need be the same procedure can be followed for introducing a third article.

When the process of adding articles to the track has been fully accomplished the 'saver' can, on occasions, be kept in the handler's pocket. The dog does not know that his favourite article is not at the end of the track but will be just as pleased to have his fun on production of the 'saver' after the last article.

The inclusion of smaller articles, especially metal or plastic ones which are less likely to hold the scent, should again be introduced whilst tracking into the wind. This approach will help you to meet with success. I always prefer to finish on a reasonable-sized article which is also well scented. It is better that the dog finishes on success rather than failure.

Some handlers believe that failure to find the last article should be countered by withholding the fun article at the end. I doubt if this form of punishment serves any useful purpose and I do not think it helps the dog next time out. This attitude generally replaces the more constructive approach of trying to reason out the cause of failure.

Dogs who are initially classified as less-motivated trackers and have been fully induced by the use of fun articles can become so dedicated to tracking that a stage may be reached when the presence of an article can become a hindrance and some may even completely ignore them. This attitude must not be allowed to take a grip and the return to larger articles with the precise knowledge of their whereabouts is essential. The use of an 'into the wind' leg with an article should help to counter the developing situation.

There can be little value in stopping a dog when he has passed the article, then taking him back to find it. This encourages a searching attitude whilst in the harness; it also breaks the concentration in a manner which may create difficulties in getting the dog back to full tracking enthusiasm. The eventual finding of this lost article also gives the handler the feeling of partial success and he may not take the failure seriously enough. It must also be remembered that on a completely blind track the handler would have no idea where the articles were placed and would have no hope of recovery.

On many competitive tracks the last article is dropped in a position where the handler can have a good idea that he has passed it and quite a number of judges allow the handlers to go back so that the dog can search for the missing article. Although I do not favour the practice I would certainly take advantage of the judge's ruling if I were competing.

Dogs will fail to find or indicate articles on occasions and there can be a number of genuine reasons: the article may be of a type which does not hold scent very well; it may not have been scented well enough by the tracklayer; it may be in a hollow or a scent trap; there may be a very strong masking scent or there may be a combination of a number of causes which have prevented a good dog from realizing that a particular article was present on the track.

However, these genuine reasons should not be used as an excuse for repeated failures. Figure 10 shows a selection of typical articles.

Fig. 10 Articles for tracking and searching.

EXPERIENCE FOR ADVANCEMENT

The groundwork for tracking has been built on enthusiasm and learning a basic routine. This gives a dog tremendous confidence in his ability to follow a scent path to its conclusion. Continued success on practice tracks will give a handler confidence and faith in his dog's ability.

Advancement on to completely blind tracks and the ability to overcome the various difficulties which make tracking such an interesting subject is very much dependent on a handler's ability to maintain enthusiasm and confidence within the partnership, also to add the third and vital ingredient — *experience.*

Experience can never be gained overnight and it takes many tracks under varying conditions with continued success to create a sound tracking dog. Although success will breed success in the future it must not be forgotten that experience of a single failure can, and will, contribute to failures in the future. If a dog has accidentally learned, on one occasion, that he can wind scent and cross over from one leg to another, he may well do it again, especially if he is in difficulty and this is the easy way out. If he has discovered that he can get out of working a difficult track by casting round and making it look as if he is working he may well do it again. It is, therefore, important that the acquisition of experience should contain the minimum of failures and the maximum respect for the cause of each failure.

BLIND TRACKS

Completely blind tracks should now become part of the build-up. These are tracks which have been laid without the dog or handler being present. The handler will be shown the starting post and may also be shown the general direction of the first leg, but otherwise he will have no further knowledge of the track and will be fully dependent on the tracklayer being present to inform him if the dog has gone wrong. These blind tracks give the handler experience and confidence, also they ensure that the dog will track on the scent of various other people. At this and later stages I still believe that most of the tracks, probably an average of three or four out of every five, should be laid by the handler or a very experienced friend.

AGEING TRACKS

The time delay between laying and working a track is generally known as the age of the track but it is sometimes quoted as being a cold track, half an hour of a time delay would be known as half an hour old or half an hour cold. Many handlers become impatient and wish to progress on to very old tracks before the dog is ready but they must realize that it takes time and practice to consolidate through the time scale.

A rough guide for ageing tracks should be based on half-hour steps. Consider tracks up to three-quarters of an hour as being within the half-hour stage, then vary tracks to a quarter of an hour on each side of one hour for the next stage.

When assessing the nature of a practice track, the age of it is only one of the factors to be considered: ground and weather conditions must also be included in the assessment before finally deciding how long to leave the track. A damp day with little wind and a field of nice, lush grass can stretch the normal one-hour track by a quarter to half an hour. A very hot, drying day, however, with a breeze combined with poor ground conditions, may well warrant a half to three-quarters of an hour-old track instead.

Inexperienced dogs may well have the scenting ability to cope with tracks older than normal but they may not appreciate that they are expected to work the older track and may use their energy trying to locate a fresher track. Some younger dogs may not have the necessary scenting ability for the older tracks, ability that maturity can give them. Both these considerations should be given due thought before trying to accelerate any tracking programme. Give an unprepared dog an hour-and-a-half track and he may work hard and complete it to your satisfaction, but give the same dog a three-month build-up from easy to progressively more difficult tracks and he will treat this hour-and-a-half track, under similar conditions, with a certain amount of contempt and make it appear to be too easy.

The combination of the age and length of a track is a factor which controls the total amount of concentration required from a dog and it is important that practice tracks should always be within the limits of the dog's powers of concentration. As an older track will probably have more than one article placed along its length a dog in difficulty should not be forced to complete the track but finish on the first available article on the track. It is much better to finish with success than to continue and court a failure.

Most experienced handlers will advise the novice not to enter a competitive stake until his dog is ready. There is no doubt that this is very sound advice, but when is a dog ready? A dog which is competent on a fifteen- to twenty-minute-old track should not encounter problems on a half-hour-old U.D. track, though a dog which is competent on a one-hour track could well have problems when faced with a track one and a half hours old, especially if the weather or ground conditions are not ideal. A handler can be put in a spot if the only convenient working trials are due before the normal process of consolidation has had time to have full effect. The question is, 'Does the handler take short cuts in preparing for the trials or does he maintain a steady programme and take a chance on the day?' He could, of course, give the trials a miss, but that is usually too high a price to pay. From my own experience a dog will lift his performance on the single occasion and give a reasonable chance of success, but the dog which has been pushed to reach the required standard is likely to falter when the chips are down. No competition should alter the planned consolidation of the practice tracks.

STARTS

An essential ingredient for success is a good start to a track. When the direction of the first leg of the track is known to the handler there should not be any problems, but practical tracking and entry in competition above the U.D. Stake leaves the handler ignorant of the direction of the track on leaving the starting post. Dog and handler should be able to approach the starting post from any direction, except the track itself, locate the scent path and choose the correct direction.

For practice tracks the tracklayer's approach, the positioning of the starting post and the direction of the first leg should be planned and discussed with the handler to ensure that variations in dog and handler approach can be applied. I would suggest, however, that the handler should plan and lay most of his own tracks or at least watch his tracklayer's start so that he knows the exact details. Misunderstanding between the tracklayer and handler has caused many a confused dog.

The routine development has encouraged the dog to put his nose to the ground in anticipation when he knows there is tracking afoot and this attitude is now invaluable. Approach the tracklayer's lead-in to the starting post into the wind so that the dog can pick up the scent. This fortifies his enthusiasm to track. The dog should be on his lead and should be allowed to track the few yards to the post. It may also be helpful to let him indicate the correct direction for a lead length beyond the post. Praise your dog, call him back and put him into harness, ready to track. You are then confident of the direction of the track.

Any tendency to back track at the start can be countered by changing the direction of your approach so that you cross the tracklayer's approach about ten yards behind the post, then circle round to make the windward approach (see Figure 11). This will create a break in the tracklayer's approach and should interrupt the dog's concentration on the back track.

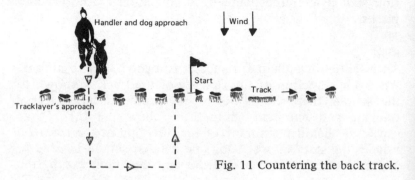

Fig. 11 Countering the back track.

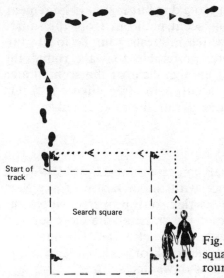

Start of track

Search square

Fig. 12 Finding a track from a square. Handler and dog progress round search square to locate track.

If he remains undecided, verbal encouragement to take the correct direction will then be required, but verbal assistance should be considered only as a last resort.

Locating a track without a starting post should also be considered and should not create any problems for a dog who is keen to start and has successfully located tracks at the lead-in to a starting post, but again the handler must initially know the exact location and direction of the first leg. It may be advisable to start by using two marker posts some fifty yards apart to indicate the line of the first leg and to introduce the dog, again into the wind, to the middle of this marked length of track. It can be very useful to educate a competitive dog in a similar manner, but without a marker. A starting post is generally left unattended for a period, especially with older tracks, and its presence seems to attract inquisitive people who invariably ruin the start of the track or who walk away with the post. Starting a track without such a marker can minimize this type of hazard.

It has also been known for a competitive track to start from a marked square, probably a twenty-five-yard search area. The area within the square will be well scented. All this scent can be very confusing to a dog but it should be remembered that there is only one scent path out from the square and that is the only part which interests you. To locate this scent path it is, therefore, preferable to walk round the outside of the square well enough clear of the scented area until the dog locates the scent path, (see Figure 12). On locating the track the harness can then be fitted so that tracking can commence.

INTERFERENCE
Game, cattle or other animals can cause untold problems on a track and gaining experience with the inclusion of any such interference can only be carried out properly when the handler has full knowledge of the track or the close support of an experienced tracklayer. How else can a handler tell whether his dog is working the track or taking an interest in the irrelevant scents from these unwanted sources?

The movement of game cannot normally be controlled but experience can be gained by laying tracks in areas where game can be expected. Rabbits are very active at first light and a few early-morning tracks in the area of their burrows will give a dog plenty of experience under such conditions. However, it can be rather inconsiderate to give a dog ageing tracks with an abundance of interference and such interference should be introduced on easy tracks where the start is expected to be reasonably clear of game. The dog should have an opportunity to settle into an enthusiastic rhythm before encountering a game-infested area.

Cattle or sheep interference can cause greater problems. Some dogs will not track in the presence of cattle and I know of some superb trackers who will not entertain such an idea. For some unknown reason other dogs will ignore their existence and track on quite regardless of their attention. Dogs who have a 'hang-up' about cattle or any other animal can only overcome this tracking problem if they can be acclimatized to their presence outside a tracking environment.

Similarly a dog who is excited by the panicky movements of a few sheep will have a problem when trying to concentrate on a track if his eyes catch their fleeting movement. Again, acclimatization outside the tracking environment is the real answer.

Cattle or sheep are continuously on the move during much of the daylight hours and to track where these animals have been can cause disastrous and discouraging failures, especially if it was not appreciated that the animals had been on the tracking ground. If your tracking ground does include the grazing of farm animals it would be wise to study their habits and movement routine.

Only experience will tell you how your dog will react to the interference scents of animals but again familiarization should be carried out with easy and relatively fresh tracks and progress be geared to the dog's acceptance of the situation.

You may find that your dog has a tendency to cast continually in areas of heavy interference. The temporary shortening of the tracking line can help minimize this casting and often gives the dog greater confidence in his abililty to overcome the problem.

It should be recognized that not all dogs have the abililty to overcome many of the problems experienced when tracking and their limitations should be met with an understanding response from the handler.

CROSS TRACKS
Human cross tracks are inevitable, especially when tracks have been left for two hours or more. Even competition ground can be contaminated with a cross track without anyone being aware of it. Although UK working trials tracking does not include intentional cross tracks at any stage, Canadian and Australian T.D.X. qualifications build this requirement into their schedule of work.

A few dogs do appear to be completely track-sure but there are occasions when even they are likely to change over onto a scent path which crosses the track they are working. As we do not know precisely the scents or odours on which a dog is concentrating, or how often he refers to the subordinate scents or odours, we do not know why he ignores or takes a cross track. Experience suggests that a dog is unlikely to take a cross track which is older than the track he is following but can well be tempted to change over to the cross track if it is fresher than the track he is following. This helps to confirm the theory that as the track gets older the dog concentrates on the ground-based odours, crushed vegetation etc., because they are stronger and easier to follow than the human scent which diminishes at a faster rate. The introduction of a fresher track with a stronger human scent brings the inherited purpose of tracking to the fore – to track for a living being.

We do not know at what stage the human scent becomes subordinate on a track; it will vary considerably and be dependent on the strength of the tracklayer's scent and the prevailing weather conditions. My own impression is that the human scents become subordinate at somewhere between half an hour and an hour old. Conditioning is based on cross tracks which are fresher than the main track although it would also be wise to assess the dog's reaction to slightly older cross tracks.

When planning the use of cross tracks there are a number of factors which must be kept in mind:

1. A dog will be tempted by a fresh human scent when the main track is old enough to have its human scent subordinate to the ground odours.
2. The distinctive scents from some people can be so much stronger and more temping than others!
3. The ground odours from a person who is heavier than the tracklayer can be an inducement to change.
4. The wind direction can be, and may well be, the most deciding factor. If a dog is tracking into the wind and the cross track scent is being carried to him, he is warned of its presence and has time to think about the value of a change. Instinct may tell him to abandon the older track. On the other hand tracking on a leg with a following wind gives the dog no warning of the cross track and if he is tracking at a good confident pace he will probably be past the cross track by a yard or so before he fully realizes its presence. Then he may well find it much more convenient to continue on the main track.

Any one of these factors, or a combination of them, can affect a dog's reliance on a track and may well explain why a dog will ignore a cross track one day and eagerly follow one on another.

Experience with cross tracks must be gained with patience. Every time the cross track has been accepted by the dog it is a failure; in a sense it is a lost track and failures in practice should be few and far between.

The introduction of any difficulty on a track should be carried out with success in mind and cross tracks are no exception. Simple tracks should be laid by the handler and probably about half an hour old; a single cross track should be sufficient. The leg of the track used for crossing should have the dog working with the wind and the cross track at right-angles. This cross track should be laid by an assistant witnessed by the handler so that he knows when to expect it. The cross track can be laid just before the dog is worked or with a time gap of up to fifteen minutes and it should intersect the track some fifty to one hundred yards from the start or from a previous corner to ensure that the dog is well settled into his work. An article some ten yards beyond the intersection can help to give a dog confidence in his decision

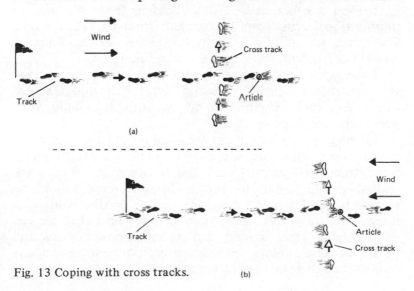

Fig. 13 Coping with cross tracks.

to ignore the cross track, or if he required help to negotiate the difficulty the article can assist in boosting his morale (see Figure 13a).

Confident in your dog's ability with a following wind, you can now include a trial when the dog is working into the wind and he has the opportunity to think about the choice before he reaches the intersection. It may be worthwhile to place a well-scented article some two or three yards beyond the intersection; the scent of this article reaching him can encourage a singleminded attitude at a crucial moment (see Figure 13b).

The best way to pin-point the exact spot of an intersection of the track and the cross track is to have the tracklayer put a post into the ground at the selected spot and have the cross tracklayer remove it as he crosses. This ensures that any article is placed at the intended distance from the cross. The successful application of cross tracks can allow the article to be placed progressively further from the intersection.

A shortage of experienced tracklayers to lay the cross tracks need not affect progress. A handler can lay his own tracks and the interference cross tracks. I have in fact laid tracks for my own dog where one leg of the track deliberately crossed another and on one occasion there was also an unintentional cross from a complete stranger with his dog. This track was fully worked by Caro when he was fourteen months old and the details are given in Figure 14.

If the same person lays the main track and the cross track there must be a tremendous temptation for the dog to accept the cross track. Continuing to use this technique must depend on the dog's reaction.

Building up on older tracks and altering the angles of intersections will conclude the normal requirements for cross track training. Reducing the angle between the cross track and the main track to about thirty degrees should be sufficient to determine the dog's ability to discriminate at intersections and the timing of cross tracks up to half the age of the main track should also be sufficient. Success and plenty of time available may, however, induce some handlers to give their dogs more exacting experience.

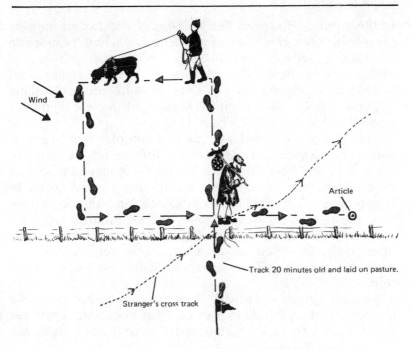

Fig. 14 Cross tracks. Note: stranger crossed track while the second leg was being worked

GROUND VARIATIONS

Dogs are asked to track on many different types of ground: heather, pasture, stubble, ploughed land or even hard surfaces such as cinder tracks or tarmacadam roads. Ground conditions can vary tremendously but the presence of good green vegetation is required to give the greatest chance of success.

Heather can normally be considered as one of the easier types of tracking ground although articles can fall through to the base and dogs not accustomed to the depth of vegetation can miss them. When a dog indicates the presence of an article which blends in with the undergrowth the handler can then have a problem in finding it.

Stubble fields become readily available after the harvest and this type of ground may initially be a problem to the inexperienced dog but vegetation seems to become evident very quickly and this improves the scent holding properties of the ground. However, the present-day practice of burning the stubble does create major problems and a high proportion of tracking failures. The lines of stubble seem to have a fascination for inexperienced dogs and practice tracks must include legs diagonal to the lines of cultivation. On these diagonal legs the dogs seem to zig-zag off the track then back on to the scent path (see Figure 15).

Tracking on ploughed land can be a completely new experience and generally creates many difficulties due to the absence of any vegetation, but the breaking-up of the surface by each footprint does release the moisture which seems to be adequate. Introduction to ploughed land should involve very fresh tracks, probably about fifteen minutes old, with progress determined by the dog's reaction. Although it is often difficult to obtain permission to track on ploughed land, the experience is a valuable addition to a dog's repertoire.

Ground spread over with farm manure seems to have a greater effect on handlers than on their dogs and experience has indicated that such rotting matter is of little consequence as a possible distraction.

If I find at any stage of tracklaying that a piece of ground is liable to create more difficulty than intended I give my feet a twist at each step to ensure greater disturbance of the soil or a more positive impression on the vegetation.

Hard-surface tracks are very much a lottery although nice, damp, cool conditions can make a half-hour time delay

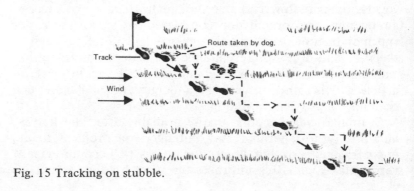

Fig. 15 Tracking on stubble.

practical. The absence of disturbed, moist soil or crushed vegetation removes the main scent- or odour-holding source and any handler should be reasonable in his expectations from a dog working under these conditions.

JUDGING

Each judge has his own approach to the responsibility he has accepted when deciding to officiate at a tracking event. It may be a simple tracking rally, an open working trials or a Championship working trials event. Whatever the standing of the event he must recognize that each competitor has put a lot of time and effort into preparing for the occasion. The organisers are also entitled to the judge's consideration, especially concerning the design of tracks which will fit into the available ground and accessibility for tracklayers moving from one track to another.

Judging at a tracking event can, therefore, be considered as a two-part function:

1.   Planning the track and selecting the articles to be used.
2.   Assessing each dog's performance on the day.

There is no standard approach to judging, although the regulations give a clear understanding of the general requirements for a specific test. Each judge will apply his own interpretation and will, therefore, formulate his own style. The details I give on judging are probably biased towards my own outlook but will no doubt be sufficiently close to that of other judges so that readers may use the information as a general guide.

Most competitive tracks are laid in fields with each containing one, two or, on occasion, three tracks. Open moorland may be used as an alternative. The use of fields normally avails the tracklayer of numerous natural landmarks as a guide and when the tracks are self-contained these fields can facilitate the more complicated track patterns. Open moorland, however, can be rather devoid of prominent landmarks and tracks should be designed to simplify the task of the tracklayer and ensure that the organisers can plan the use of their ground to minimize wastage and yet still keep a reasonable distance between each track.

A judge must also give the tracklayer a certain amount of discretion to modify the lengths of each leg on a track to ensure that the ground available can accommodate the basic features of his track.

The shape of a track or its important features will be determined by the grade of competition. Does a judge intend to make a difficult start to the track? Does he wish to test the partnership half-way round or in the final section? A difficult start can mean a complete, or almost complete, failure with minimal marks being awarded. This is quite in order but will be very discouraging to a beginner in the lower grades in competition. A track should be designed to give a good dog a fair chance of qualifying although certain features can be included to help sort out the top dogs, or even to determine the handler's ability to trust his dog.

The selection of articles should be dependent on the type of ground being used and also the grade of competition. Articles do not need to be small to compensate for lack of undergrowth but can be selected to blend in with the prevailing conditions. They may, however, be deliberately chosen to be more obvious to the eye but could be mistaken for a piece of discarded waste. It is with the tracklayer's co-operation that the dog should easily locate and indicate the presence of the article. There should be little chance of the handler recognizing the article without the dog's assistance.

The allocation of marks for any section of a track should be related to the complexity of that section. The fact that the dog registers the start of the track and completes the first ten yards means that it is probably worth more than any other ten-yard section of the track. The fact that a dog negotiates an acute-angled corner means that he has shown greater expertise than negotiating an obtuse-angled corner and it may be worth varying the marks for these corners. A guide for a distribution of the marks can be approximated from the following percentages of the total marks allocated to the track:

Starting the track — 5%
Each corner   — 2% to 4%
Remainder at x marks per 100 yards

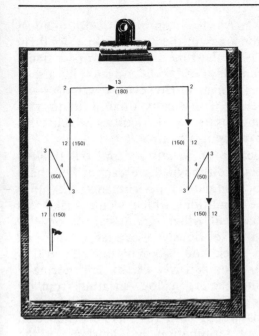

Fig. 16 Example of a
competition track.
Length of each leg
shown in yards in brackets.
Start: 5 marks. Six
corners: 16 marks.
Approximately 8
marks per hundred
yards. Total: 90 marks.

An example track for W.D. Stake is illustrated in Figure 16, where 90 marks are allocated in the schedule. A possible breakdown shows the allocation to the start, the corners and each leg according to its length.

Any form of marking can only be a guide and a change within an individual track to accommodate the ground which is available will require a modification of the marks to suit.

Assessing a dog and handler's performance on a track is purely subjective and can only relate to a judge's sense of justice. A judge must assess whether there were reasonable grounds for a cast or not and should only deduct marks where he feels that the dog is not applying himself properly. Every dog who completes a full track has earned his marks and each deviation, be it a cast or an investigation, must be related to the application of the partnership before marks are deducted. Any lack of canine concentration or faulty handling should not go unpunished and must cost the partnership the appropriate number of marks.

There is always a measure of regret when a dog has to be

called off the track, he may have been in difficulties or just too slow to complete the track in the allotted time. As there is no hard and fast rule on the time taken to work a track, the allotted period is generally set by the judge on his assessment of a reasonable performance. However, few judges will stick to the allotted period if a worthy qualifier requires a little extra time to compensate for difficulties which were probably outside the partnership's control.

To be called off because of deviation from the track is quite another problem and although there cannot be a hard and fast rule when to terminate a performance the judge must keep in mind the conditions which would make this action essential and base all other circumstances on this judgment. Termination is obviously essential if the dog deviates from his own track and is going to foil another competitor's track. As competitive tracks are normally seventy-five yards or more apart, a dog deviating from his own track by fifty yards could expect to have his performance terminated. This would be a reasonable distance in any direction to warrant termination and marking of the track up to the point of deviation.

A judge often feels that to let a dog continue whilst he is having real trouble on or close to the track will do more harm than good and that he should terminate the performance. Although the intention is commendable, many a handler has complained when this has been done, saying that he was about to retrieve the situation. It is much safer for a judge to wait until the dog has deviated a suitable distance or the partnership has been given the full period of time for the track. Some handlers, with reservations about their dog's ability, will ask the judge to call them off the track under such circumstances.

The greatest satisfaction after judging a tracking event, is to sit back in a fireside chair, recollect the top performances and marvel at the expertise of this canine inheritance.

8

Free Tracking

Free tracking is the term used when a dog is permitted to track without any physical restrictions, no tracking harness and line to help maintain an acceptable pace. This can be in the form of forward tracking where the dog is following the scent path in the same direction as the tracklayer and this is generally termed FREE TRACKING On the other hand the dog could purposely be sent to track in the opposite direction to the tracklayer, to find out where he has come from and this is generally known as the SEEK BACK.

These tracks are normally worked when they are very fresh, generally immediately after they have been laid and any dog with enthusiasm for the game can partake and enjoy himself. The free track is normally used to find a hidden person and the seek back can be applied to find an article dropped some distance back by the handler.

Both kinds of free tracking can be enjoyed by all members of the family and will give both children and adults a great deal of fun whilst the dogs will find the mental and physical exercise very stimulating.

Free tracking and the seek back were working trials competitive exercises in days gone by. The free track was dropped because it seemed to lack practical value and the seek back was replaced by the more practical search exercise. It would appear that of the English-speaking countries, only the Australian obedience schedule includes any form of the free track and this is the seek back detailed in their Utility Class.

As free tracking and the seek back can bring so much enjoyment into the life of the family pet I feel that they are worthy of inclusion in this book.

FREE TRACKS

Although free tracking can be used to find articles the greatest fun can be obtained when your dog is released to find a member of the family. It is a form of hide-and-seek which can be enjoyed by the children.

The basic principle of tracking inducements comes to the fore; the dog will not be interested unless there is some inducement with the feeling of reward or satisfaction at the end of it. The dog may not be interested if his favourite member of the family is releasing him to look for another, but change the roles and see the effect. The inducement principles required for free tracking are similar to those explained for line tracking in chapter 7, especially the induce-ment by ˙food˙ described ˙on˙ pages 65-66. This, of course, would be without the lead and the dog would be released to run ahead to find the tracklayer.

The use of the phrase, 'You find him, son', or a physical gesture or even both on every occasion you release the dog to go and find your tracklayer will ensure that he will eventually understand your requirements without the stimulus of seeing the tracklayer go off to hide.

SEEK BACK

There is no doubt that the seek back can be a most useful function. A glove, a bunch of keys or any such possession dropped accidentally whilst out for a walk can easily be retrieved by a dog suitably trained. As a game, the seek back will certainly help to convince any family pet that he is an asset to the household and he will relish the opportunity to use his nose for such a carefree activity.

The principle is to have your dog reacting to the use of a phrase, a gesture, or both, so that he will retrace the route you have just walked to find an article you dropped on the way. This may have been twenty yards back, or a hundred yards or even half a mile, if your dog has been trained to retrace your footsteps for such a distance.

Again we proceed from retrieving by sighting the article when changing over to scenting and we make use of a keen, enthusiastic retrieve of a fun article to achieve the desired result. Start by having fun with your dog and his favourite article, put him on his lead and let him see you drop the article as you run forward with him for a suitable distance, say ten to twenty yards. Turn round and release your dog with encouragement to retrieve the article. At this stage, it will not matter if the article is in full view, you wish to have him appreciate that you are releasing him to retrieve his article. You are not telling him to go back, nor are you commanding him to return but you are releasing him to go back for his article, because he wants to go back for it. You can make some kind of encouraging gesture with a suitable phrase. I use 'Where is it, son, you go and get it!' It is the use of that gesture or phrase which will finally let him know that you have dropped the article en route.

Extend the distance to some fifty yards or so and on occasions drop the article in longer grass or the undergrowth so that he will not see the article until he has located it by scent. At this stage keep him on the lead until you have walked a suitable distance before releasing him.

When you feel that your dog is likely to respond, drop the article where it will be clearly in sight, but without him noticing the actual drop. Walk on some twenty yards, turn and use your releasing gesture, phrase or both, and watch for his reaction. If his reaction is not strong enough walk back with him and, with encouragement, get him to retrieve the article. Your dog should catch on fairly quickly but if not, spend a bit more time working at the elementary stage. A satisfactory response, however, should result in the build-up with the surreptitious drop. On occasions use conditions which will keep the article from view until your dog is right on top of it.

The scent of your track will be very strong and your dog is unlikely to work exactly on top of your footprints, especially with a cross wind. A broad scent path will give him plenty of scope and any attempt on your part to gain greater accuracy will probably end up with an unenthusiastic worker. Just let him work naturally.

Your article for training will be dual-scented, contaminated with your own and your dog's scent. Try him with a change of article, with your scent only, but drop it surreptitiously in the open so that he can see the article as he gets closer to it. Use a glove or something of a similar size, then let him get accustomed to various other articles. Make sure the article is well-scented, your dog may be travelling at quite a pace when he passes it and you do not want him to overshoot to the extent that he will miss the article.

When your dog can seek back on a straight line some fifty to a hundred yards long include an obtuse-angled corner or a bend, but preferably when he is seeking back into the wind (see Figure 17a). Gradually make the corner more acute until the right-angle has been achieved. Try him with the wind in varying directions but expect him to overshoot the corners on occasions; it is his keenness to recover the track which really matters.

Your dog may have a tendency to cut across corners when the wind blows the scent of the other leg towards him but this habit can be avoided if the article is usually dropped just after you have turned a corner (see Figure 17b). Your dog will soon understand that he must seek back on your tracks to be sure of finding the article.

A good, keen dog will soon learn to seek back through two, three or more corners and can give endless enjoyment to the family.

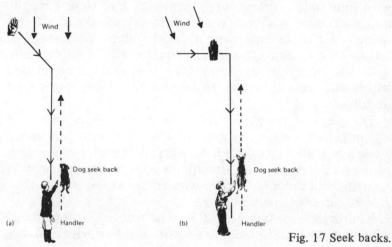

Fig. 17 Seek backs.

The usefulness of the seek back in a domestic situation was recalled to me by Miss Moncreiffe of Moncreiffe. Some years ago the seek back was included in the working trials schedule and Miss Moncreiffe's young German Shepherd bitch, Zara, who was the foundation of her now famous Dunmonaidh prefix, had been trained to the working trials routine.

On this occasion, however, Miss Moncreiffe and Zara had accompanied her brother, Sir David, for a round of golf on the renowned course at Gleneagles in Scotland when she discovered, at the eighteenth green, that her headscarf was missing. She had obviously dropped it somewhere on the course.

Miss Moncreiffe asked Zara to 'Go, seek and find it' and to the astonishment of the caddy, Zara set off to retrace the steps of the trio. She must have back tracked nearly half the length of the golf course to find the scarf then promptly returned with it by the shortest route to the utter amazement of the wide-eyed caddy.

This superb piece of nosework was really very simple for a dog who was trained as well as being willing and eager to please her mistress.

9

Scent Discrimination

INTRODUCTION

Scent discrimination is an exercise which is carried out as part of the working schedule in obedience competitions and, within the various English-speaking countries, this exercise seems to be based on either the British system or the American approach.

The British system provides for a graduation through three different stages of competition from a relatively simple test giving scope for the use of a dual-scented article, scented by dog and handler, to one bearing the scent of a stranger to the dog. The American approach is based on a single, middle-of-the-road exercise where two different types of material are used and the articles to be located and retrieved carry the handler's scent only.

The general approach to training which is described in this chapter will be based on the British competition requirements with additional information being given to cover the variations within the American exercise.

Scent discrimination can also be a very enjoyable party trick for the domestic pet who can have friends amazed at his ability to pick out the correct article. A few examples will be given at the end of the chapter.

If a handler wishes to compete in both obedience and working trials special precautions must be taken to ensure that the dog understands the difference between scent discrimination and the search exercise which follows in Chapter 10. Although scent discrimination starts with a very free and easy introduction it is developed through to an exercise of precision. The search exercise can maintain a less formal approach and gives the handler more scope to apply a completely different attitude. I hope this will become evident in the differences within the relevant chapters.

THE EXERCISE

The purpose of this exercise is to have the dog discriminate between articles which have been handled by different people, to locate and retrieve the article carrying the scent of the selected person. The three stages of competition have a natural progression from one to another and this leads to a sensible approach to training. The competition stages are:

1 *Class A* The handler's own article is used with the handler's scent on it and it is placed amongst a variety of different articles. At least one of the other articles will carry the scent of some person other than the handler.
2 *Class B* An article supplied by the judge and bearing the handler's scent is placed amongst similar articles where the dog cannot visually recognize the correct one. Again at least one of the other articles should carry the scent of some person other than the handler.
3 *Class C* On this ocasion pieces of cloth are used, about six inches square, and the dog is required to discriminate and return with the piece which has been handled by the judge. Again at least one of the other cloths should be scented by some person other than the judge or the handler.

The procedure for each stage of competition is the same. The articles, up to a maximum of ten, are placed on the ground some two feet apart to a pattern determined by the judge. The articles should be clearly visible to the dog and probably about five to ten paces from the handler. The steward will take an article from the handler and, without putting his own scent on it, place it amongst the other articles whilst the handler prevents the dog from watching the article being placed. In Class A and Class B the scent of the article to be located is normally given to the dog by the handler cupping his hands over the dog's nose so that he can associate the handler's scent with the article he must select from the group. In Class C, a cloth with the judge's scent is usually draped over the dog's nose so that he can memorize the stranger's scent. In each case the dog is released with the instruction to go out and investigate the articles laid out on the ground then return with the appropriate article.

To save any confusion when reading this chapter the various articles used in scent discrimination will now be clearly defined.

The word 'article' will be used to indicate the scented one which should be located and returned by the dog. All others will be known as 'objects' although the individual objects which have been deliberately scented by other people and should be ignored by the dog will be referred to as 'decoys'. Reference will also be made to articles which are 'dual-scented'; these are articles which have been touched by the handler and also previously retrieved by the dog, thereby carrying scent from the handler's hands and also saliva from the dog's mouth. With dual-scented articles we do not know whether it is the handler's scent or the dog's own scent which is being used for identification. I presume that the dog's own scent is the more prominent and will be the true inducement to retrieve the article.

The competitive scent discrimination exercise must be conducted in the manner expected of all others in the obedience schedule of work. Every movement, from start to finish, should be performed with smartness and precision. It is not my intention within this chapter to detail the training requirements for such precision, as this can be considered to be part of the general training required for the competitive retrieve exercise. My intention is to detail the principles of scent discrimination and a method of progressing through each stage from a straightforward retrieve to the Class C scenting requirements so that a dog will continually work with purpose in his mind.

A dog should not be introduced into this field of work unless he is a good keen retriever. Discriminating to the levels of Class A and B is relatively easy for a dog to understand if he has a keen desire to retrieve, but to attempt the schooling for this routine with a dog who lacks the enjoyment of a pleasant and smart retrieve is to encourage most of the bad habits which can be picked up at many of the training classes.

DEVELOPING THE ROUTINE AND CLASS A SCENTING
The Class A routine sets the pattern and establishes the foundation for the more advanced exercises. Any faults which have been allowed to develop in this class of work will be difficult to eradicate during the more advanced stages.

Scent discrimination is a SIGHT and SCENT exercise in which the dog visually locates the group of scattered objects then identifies the correct article from within the group by scenting as required.

The pattern of association should, therefore, be developed with a well-used retrieve article, one the dog enjoys and with which he is perfectly capable of accomplishing a sound retrieve. If the dog is not proficient in the retrieve exercise it would be harmful and foolish to try and improve the finer points of retrieving during the sessions of schooling for scent discrimination. A dog who mouths an article, plays around or pounces on it will only become confused if he is corrected for these faults during scent practice. The situation must be developed where no unpleasantness can be connected in his mind with the business of scent discrimination.

Many of the retrieving problems to be overcome at this stage can be caused by the over-excitement of certain natural retrievers. Border Collies seem to be more susceptible than other breeds to this over-excited condition and many are liable to scatter everything before them whilst carrying out the scenting exercise. This is decidedly a retrieving problem; it must be treated as such and brought under control before attempting to develop the scenting routine. I repeat that the important point with any dog is to solve all retrieving problems first and Class A scent will fall into place very quickly.

Discriminating between objects to find the article bearing his handler's scent is one of the most natural functions for any dog and to discriminate for an article which also bears his own scent can only simplify the task still further. Any family pet who enjoys a retrieve will search a pebbled beach for the particular stone his master threw for him and he will not be interested in bringing back any other. A piece of wood thrown in the same manner whilst walking through a wood will meet with a similar response. Yet these family pets have not been given the scent by their owner. They already know his scent and no self-respecting dog will mistake another scent for that of his master.

It is only when we turn this natural function into an artificial exercise that we create 'hang-ups' in the minds of our dogs. The purpose of this development of a routine is to make the change so casual that the dog does not realize that he is being asked to carry out an artificial exercise and he still thinks of it as a natural function. A number of dogs do achieve a successful scenting and retrieve at the very first attempt if initially presented with the artificial conditions related to a competition set-up. These dogs have a natural ability and the preliminaries may be quite unnecessary although practice will be required to consolidate on the routine.

The first step in the routine is to make use of a well-liked retrieve article which the dog can recognize by sight as his own. Although a dumb-bell can be used at first it cannot be used in competition so it would be preferable to start with some other article of your dog's choice. This will be dual-scented, bearing his scent as well as your own. He should already be prepared to retreive this article from anywhere, long grass, heavy undergrowth or any area where junk can be lying around. It is an article he will search for until it is found.

Have a number of objects, about six or seven should be sufficient, of a similar size or larger than your own article, scattered widely on the ground some four to six feet apart. These objects should be clearly visible to the dog and must not carry your own scent. Old shoes, gloves or such like which may be used must not be your own, no matter how long it has been since you were in contact with them, and it is preferable that a stranger or a friend place the objects for you. It is wise to introduce early on decoy objects which have been well-handled and thereby scented, to ensure that your dog is acclimatized to this type of distraction from the start. If on occasion you do not have a friend available to put the objects out for you, you can do this yourself so long as you do not touch them — make use of a pair of tongs. It may also be important that your dog does not see you place the objects — even without your scent on them he may connect you with them.

During the development of this routine it is not necessary to give your dog the scent from cupped hands round his nose to accomplish the exercise; he already knows that your scent will be on the article. The cupping of your hands gently round his nose is only to prepare him for the more advanced scenting exercises to come and this can be introduced into the routine at a stage when it is felt that the action will not affect his performance. Commands should also be avoided, with gentle phrases being used to express your requirements and also your pleasure. These phrases should include the key word which will eventually become the single-worded command required for a competition performance. For example, the final word of instruction can initially be incorporated in the phrase 'Good boy, you go and seek for it' until eventually a gentle but positive 'seek' will suffice.

To commence your schooling maintain a casual approach, as if you were about to give your dog a fun retrieve, and throw the article beyond the objects on the ground (see Figure 18). Look for and expect a normal retrieve under these conditions. If he has to search round and sniff at any of the objects to check them out it shows that he is discriminating, so long as he is continually working to find his article you have no cause for complaint.

Now have the objects placed closer together, two or three feet apart, so that they indicate a more definite area of distinctive objects, and throw your article amongst them whilst your dog is watching. Hold your dog until the article has landed and is stationary before releasing him for another fun retrieve. As the objects have been handled by somebody else he may well discriminate before returning with the correct article. Some dogs will only use their nose when their eyes cannot identify their own articles, others are more at

Fig. 18 Preparing for the basic Class A routine.

home using their olfactory system and prefer to identify in this manner, even if the visual evidence is perfectly clear.

Success and complete satisfaction at this stage can encourage you to have the article placed in amongst the other objects whilst your dog is watching. You may on occasions wish to break his vision for a few seconds, by moving in front of him or turning him round in a complete circle then letting him go out for his article. This momentary break of visual contact makes a dog lose sight of his article but the knowledge of its general location is sufficient incentive to go and seek it out in the correct area. It is important, however, that the routine becomes firmly implanted in his mind and that he is required to investigate the area of visible objects to locate the article he is trying to find.

To hide the article behind one of the larger objects will soon show just how much your dog does depend on his nose. Failure to work for his article would indicate that he is not ready and requires greater confidence on sighting the article.

When retrieving the article after each discrimination your dog deserves genuine and freely given praise. If titbits are a help make use of them but remember that food taken from the hand will add a third major scent to the article if it is used again. In the early stages there is nothing wrong with this third scent so long as its presence is acknowledged by the handler.

Although it has been suggested that the development of the routine should be conducted with a single and special retrieve article a choice of such articles could be used so long as the dog does not become confused. If a single article has been used in the past the introduction of others can be made by going back to an earlier sighting stage.

To return with the wrong article when applying the handler's scent is the biggest crime in this exercise, but not a crime where the dog is blamed and punished. It indicates a failure in the process of education and if such an error does occur the dog should not be made to feel that he has done wrong but the correct article should be retrieved by the handler and immediately followed by a fun retrieve from within the scenting area. Consideration must then be given to the cause of the failure and the prevention of others.

With consistent success the Class A scenting exercise can be gradually perfected to the competition requirements. As with any other exercise excess participation during any one session will do more harm than good; some dogs 'go off' after two scents, even in the early stages, but others can take more. It is up to each handler to determine his dog's limitations and stop before he reaches that stage.

CLASS B SCENTING

Whilst competing in this grade of work the handler will never know the type of article which is likely to be used until the day of the show. The variety of articles used from show to show can be exceedingly numerous; they can be made of metal, wood, paper, fabric, plastic, leather or many other materials, they can also be presented in any shape or form. It will, therefore, be evident that a very versatile retriever will be required, a dog who is prepared to retrieve anything at the whim of his handler. To enter Class B scent with anything less may well convert an excellent Class A scent dog into a confused and unpredictable performer.

I cannot emphasize too strongly the need to acquire versatility in retrieving before considering the competition requirements of this exercise.

So long as your dog has this versatility, there is no need to practise scenting with a great number of different types of article. When it is considered that approximately a dozen identical pieces are required to ensure that a sufficient number may be scattered on the ground as objects, the remainder are used individually as the scented articles to be located and retrieved. Remember that as soon as an article has been in your dog's mouth it has become dual-scented and it may well be his own scent which attracts him to the article if it is used on future scenting. Most articles can, however, be washed to remove the scent from a previous application.

The preparation for a Class B scent can now be based on a three-phased programme:

1. A plain sighting fun retrieve of a scent article when it is thrown into an area adjacent to similar objects which have been set out for scent discrimination (see Figure 19a).

2. Scent discrimination of a dual-scented article which has been placed into the discrimination set-up. It may initially be advisable to let your dog see the article being placed to ensure success (see Figure 19b).

3. The personal scenting on a fresh article which is then placed into the discrimination area. Again it may be advisable at first to let your dog see the article being placed. Remember that success breeds success and failure encourages confusion.

The discrimination set-up need not involve the full quota of objects and articles as specified in the competition

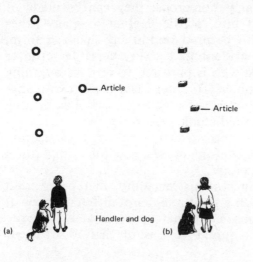

(a)   Handler and dog   (b)   Fig. 19 Visual aids to scenting.

schedule and it may be advisable in practice to start with two to four objects to make it simple, with additional objects being included as you and your dog become more confident.

Decoys, the objects which are scented by other people, can be introduced at any stage but I feel that the earlier they are admitted into the discrimination set-up the easier it is for the dog. Decoys in the scenting area during the stage of dual-scenting your article are likely to show that they will be ignored and their place in the set-up accepted as uninteresting objects. It is the handler's objective to ensure that these decoys remain uninteresting during the whole scenting life of the dog.

The position of the decoys and the scents being used can be varied, but in a competitive line-up there are seldom more than two decoy objects and possibly two different decoy scents. The decoys can be positioned so that the dog is likely to pass over at least one before reaching the scented article. It may be placed at the head of a line-up or next in line to the handler's scented article.

Competitive set-ups vary considerably but there are five basic patterns which can be used to prepare the dog for any pattern a judge may think of using (see Figure 20). These patterns are:

1. A single line of ten pieces.
2. A double line some four feet apart, five pieces in each.
3. Shape of a letter H.
4. Shape of a letter Y.
5. Pieces in a circle.

The scented article may be placed within the general formation of the pattern or it may be placed on its own within the general scenting area. One common practice is to find the article placed in the centre of a circle of objects. Some dogs will go round and round the objects and never locate the obvious article in the centre.

Schooling for Class B and the more advanced Class C should therefore be based on having your dog go out to investigate the obvious first.

In the earlier stages place your article in an obvious

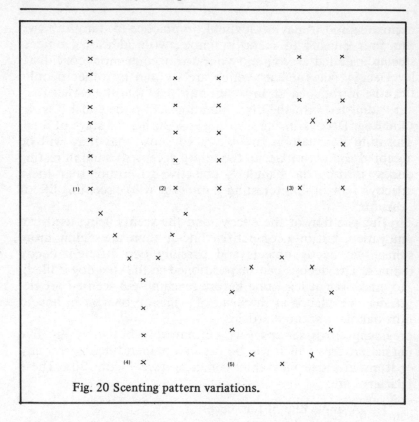

Fig. 20 Scenting pattern variations.

position and let him see it, this will bring a straight forward retrieve, but do not do it too often, just sufficient to have him curious of the isolated and obvious. On occasions use an unscented object to draw your dog to the obvious before he goes on to discriminate for his article within the main group. However, if you are to use a decoy as the obvious, first place your scented article within six to twelve inches of it to minimize the risk of him returning with the decoy just because it is more obvious and scented.

The regulations make it perfectly clear that, in competition, the article must not be given to the dog prior to the test as this would create a dual-scented situation. It is well known, however, that some handlers counter the spirit of this regulation by pretending to fondle their dogs whilst they remove saliva from the dog's mouth with their finger-tips, then they proceed to dual-scent the article before handing it to the steward. This practice may help to guarantee success at this level of competition but will do nothing to prepare the dog for the critical change-over to that of a stranger's scent in Class C.

CLASS C SCENTING

This is the ultimate in scent discrimination, to have your dog accept and memorize the scent of a stranger, then go out to a display of scent cloths and return with the matching scented article.

As all scenting to date has been accomplished on articles carrying the handler's scent this change, to that of a stranger, requires a great deal of consideration. It is not a single easy step up from Class B scent but a series of small steps graduated to ensure a smooth change-over.

I make no apologies for repeating the emphasis on the retrieve aspect of scenting because I have seen dogs being introduced to the Class C scent routine when they have not previously been asked to retrieve the various types of scenting material used in this grade of competition.

It must be remembered that your dog has been conditioned to ignore the scents of strangers. Now we wish to have him concentrate on the scent of a particular stranger and at the same time to ignore the scents of other strangers during that particular discriminating session.

The manner in which the dog has been given scent to discriminate for the handler's scented article can now be developed further to ensure that he understands the scent on which he is expected to concentrate. A cloth bearing the scent of the person in question can be placed over the dog's nose; this is the most common approach to giving the dog a particular scent and is probably the best method to use during the early period of tuition. Some handlers find that dangling the cloth in front of the dog's nose, or having it dropped on the ground so that he may pick it up, are quite acceptable methods for memorizing scent, but I would suggest that these methods be ignored until the dog is reasonably experienced.

The new experience of giving a stranger's scent by means of a piece of cloth may well cause a certain amount of apprehension and this can create a mental block which could affect the dog's ability to memorize and, therefore, to discriminate. This apprehension can easily be overcome, by introducing cloth scenting with the handler using his own scent as in Class A and Class B and developing to the other scents only when the dog is perfectly happy to accept this procedure.

The introduction of other scents can now be considered and one must appreciate the reaction of a dog to being given a different scent. Does he know what is expected of him? Will he connect the scented article with the scent he has been given? It is not a question of memorizing the scent, but a question of relating one scent to the other.

The process of discrimination should be made so easy that the dog has only a minimal chance of going wrong. The assistance of another member of the household, or a friend who is well known to the dog will simplify the process. If you use a person who is well known to your dog he does not really require to memorize his scent, your dog knows it already. These friends or relatives will now become your scenting assistants. These assistants should not have been previously used for decoy scenting, nor should they be used for that purpose in the future, at least not until the dog is quite experienced and fully understands the requirements of the test. I am sure that many dogs become confused because they are expected to bring back an article bearing a particular scent at one training session then they are expected to ignore the same scent as a decoy during the next session.

A return to dual-scenting of articles can help a dog to become accustomed to bringing back articles with your assistant's scent as the subordinate scent and the dog's own scent as the real inducement to pick up the correct cloth. Although dual-scented articles were described earlier in this chapter as articles bearing the scent of the handler and that of the dog we can now consider the term to apply to that of the scenting assistant and the dog. Every effort should be made to ensure that the handler's scent is not being transmitted to the dog instead of his assistant's.

Sighting should also play its part in assisting your dog to identify the correct cloth in the early stages. Have your assistant scent two cloths by rubbing them in his hands. Having them in his pocket for a period or breathing on them will also help to leave a heavy scent. Your assistant will require additional cloths and these can be kept in his pocket until required. Take one of the scented cloths, handle it by the top corners only and place it over your dog's nose. At the same time your assistant should draw attention to himself as he drops the other scented cloth on the ground some ten paces away. He then steps back as you remove the cloth from your dog's nose and release him to retrieve the cloth. Take the retrieved cloth from your dog in a manner which will minimize the effect of your own scent and return it to your assistant for re-scenting.

The scenting cloth used to put over the dog's nose will now be contaminated with the scent from your own hands and should not be used again. A freshly scented cloth from your assistant will be required.

Have one to three cloths suitably placed on the ground by a third party, then your scenting assistant can place his dual-scented cloth beside the others whilst your dog is watching. If necessary have your assistant draw the dog's attention to his activities. Place the freshly scented cloth over your dog's nose for a few seconds and again release him to find your assistant's dual-scented cloth. Repeat the process with two freshly scented cloths to see if your dog can achieve success without the aid of his own scent.

Some dogs catch on very quickly and do not require the inducement of dual-scented cloths whilst others take some time before they fully understand your requirements. It is simply a case of adjusting your approach to suit your dog. Dual-scented cloths may be used two or three times between washes. The heavy contamination with saliva from a dog's mouth after a few applications may well mask your assistant's scent to the degree that it is meaningless to the dog. The additional cloths placed on the ground by the third party should be slightly decoy-scented. This gives a background of human scent to each cloth without being particularly distinctive and attractive to your dog. Success through practice can influence your decision on when to increase the strength of decoy scents.

Progress to the full exercise with ten cloths can be planned by building up to single-scented cloths from one assistant then returning to the earliest stage with a fresh assistant and then repeating the full process with other assistants until your dog is fully competent with any of four to six different assistants. The alternative is to carry out the full elementary stages with a variety of scenting assistants before progressing with each assistant in turn until the full exercise has been accomplished with single-scented cloths.

As the various patterns for setting out scent discrimination objects and articles have been fully discussed in preparing for Class B, the experience with cloths in similar patterns will not create any problems. It should be remembered, however, that the related variables discussed for Class B scent should be included in the Class C routine.

The work involved in continually washing and drying used cloths to remove all scent can be minimized by making use of kitchen paper towelling or paper handkerchiefs during practice sessions, especially beyond the stage of dual-scenting.

OTHER SCENTING CONSIDERATIONS
So far this chapter has been concerned with the build-up of a routine to ensure that a dog can be quite capable of interpreting his handler's scent discrimination requirements and carrying out this function to his satisfaction. There are, however, a number of unknowns which may well affect advanced scenting and competition at the level of Class C.

The atmosphere round the scenting cloths will contain an infinite variety of scents and odours with differing degrees of concentration. Although these atmospheric conditions should not have any effect on Class A or B scents, where the handler's personal scent is known to the dog, the stranger's scent used in Class C can change the nature of the exercise to a degree that this pollution of scents in the atmosphere can, on occasions, prove too great an obstacle for the dogs and for handlers less capable of coping with the complexities of such varied conditions.

A selection of such possible conditions follows:

1. The presence of other human beings in the general vicinity of the working area will create a mixture of body scents in the atmosphere. Their clothes and footwear will also add to the composition of the atmospheric ingredients.

2. Other dogs at the training class or show will also make their contribution and can have a distracting influence, especially if there is a bitch just coming into, or just out of season.

3. Odours from the composition of the floor or its surface, be it polish, a sealant or a disinfectant cleaner, may possibly add to the general accumulation within the atmosphere. These odours will be at their strongest at ground level, where the cloths have been placed for the exercise.

4. Outdoor venues in a playing-field can create a different set of conditions with the effect of handlers, dogs, steward and judge trampling over the grass causing extensive bruising and crushing of vegetation. If a dog can track a single set of footprints hours after a person has walked over such a piece of ground, I hate to think of the strength and variety of odours created within a typical obedience ring.

5. Incidental scents from a decoy steward which may match with those of the judge may well cause confusion. The use of soaps, hand creams or even facial cosmetics of the same brand may have a misleading effect.

Many of these scents or odours will be of little significance but others may well be much stronger than the prime scent on the cloth which is intended for discrimination. One or more of these subordinate scents may tend to mask or distort the prime scent sufficiently to mislead the dog with a less sensitive olfactory system or one which lacks the concentration to match the scent given with the correct cloth.

All of these factors can give the ill-prepared a mountain of excuses for failure but they must also be recognized as possible contributing factors to the unexplained failure from a good, well-educated scent discriminator.

Another more decisive factor can be the similarity of scents between one individual and another. Although in theory each person carries a distinctive scent, how distinctive are all of these individual scents? There are fifty million people in the UK and all with distinctive scents: two hundred million in the United States and six hundred million Chinese with each person emitting a distinctive scent. Are there really so many individual scents that a dog can differentiate between each and every one?

I remember stewarding at a Championship Class C event when two young ladies were recruited as scent decoy stewards. Their function was to scent cloths by rubbing them in their hands. The discrimination cloths were in a straight line and decoy steward A would place her cloth first in the line so that each dog would have the opportunity of checking it out on his way down the line. The judge had her cloth placed half-way down the line and decoy steward B would place hers at the far end of the line. The scented cloths were changed for each dog to ensure that the decoys' and the judge's cloths all carried scent of the same age. Approximately half of the dogs returned to their handlers with the correct cloth whilst the other half returned with the decoy from steward B. No cloths bearing the scent of steward A were brought in by any dog.

A statistical significance test involving the entry of twenty-four dogs would show conclusively that there was a bit more than the laws of chance involved here and I believe that the failures, who were proven scent workers, honestly believed that the decoy scent B was the scent they were given from the judge's second cloth. We have heard tales of this kind before, from other shows where an abnormally high failure rate occurs. Sometimes it is just an excuse from the handler of an ill-prepared dog but top dogs in their prime are known to suffer the same fate.

I have discussed earlier in chapter 6 the probability of

human scent groupings, as with fingerprints, blood and saliva groupings. Was it a case of decoy scent steward B and the judge coming from the same scent group, and closely related within this group? Were the scents so closely related that the pollution of other odours, especially from crushed vegetation immediately below the cloths, had masked that minor difference? (See Figure 21.) Or perhaps the judge and steward had washed their hands with the same brand of soap, or they may have applied the same type of hand-cream. I do not know the answer but it does pose an interesting question.

I have also heard of a case where there was a high failure rate and eventually the judge and decoy steward discovered they were both pipe smokers and enjoyed the same brand of tobacco.

Consider each group of scents as a colour in the spectrum. What an infinite variety of combinations and shades can be seen by the human eye. One shade can be very close to another and one dash of primary colour can make a distinctive difference to a shade. Can we relate those fifty million human scents in the UK to this infinite variety of colours and shades?

It should also be remembered that a dog is working from memory; he must memorize the scent he is given and match it with one from a selection of scents. Consider our own limitations with memorizing a visual identification. Each person looks different, but is there such a difference within like groups without their distinctive clothing or hair-styles, etc? How often do police identity-parades fail because people of a certain likeness are brought together and all in similar

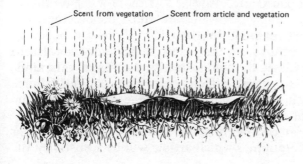

Fig. 21 Effects of odours from crushed vegetation.

clothing? How many of us choose to dial a strange telephone number without having it written in front of us? To walk from one room to another with a memorized telephone number is often sufficient to have some of us doubt our powers of retaining numerical information.

These considerations may not be of any consequence when decoy and judge's scents are distinctively different, but minor differences could be masked by one or more of the many subordinate scents and odours which hang around a scenting area. A dog's memory and his keenness to satisfy could well result in a case of mistaken identity.

Armed with these theories a judge and his ring steward can only set out to minimize the subordinate scents and give each dog a reasonable chance of success. Any planning decisions are likely to be a compromise; after all it is supposed to be a practical exercise and completely sterile conditions would be out of the question. I would, therefore, suggest that the following points be given some consideration:

1. Minimize the amount of traffic within the area to be used for the scent cloths, particularly for outdoor shows where crushed vegetation can give off the most prominent odour. Remember how sweet newly-mown grass can smell to the human senses.
2. As there is quite a strong opinion that human male scent is always distinctively different from that of a female it may be advisable to chose decoy stewards of the opposite sex to that of the judge.
3. Check on the subordinate human scents: soap, hand cream, tobacco, etc.

AMERICAN SCENT DISCRIMINATION
The principal features of this exercise are very similar to those of the Class B scent already discussed. There is, however, one important difference which can affect the general approach to the schooling of the exercise and the competitive application.

The articles in competition are provided by the handler and the judge determines which article will be scented by the handler and retrieved by his dog. The full details relating to this exercise and the approach to marking have been extracted from the American Kennel Club Obedience Regulations and are given in Appendix 3 (see page 190). As the handler supplies all the bits and pieces it is very important that none of them carries his scent prior to their presentation to the judge.

Again the preparation for this exercise necessitates a good, sound, happy retrieve with the types of articles to be used. Remember that the articles are the handler's own choice, so long as one type is of a metal base and the other of leather.

Dual-scenting can again be the basis for schooling the routine and the three-phased application described in the Class B section can also be followed.

Although the metal and leather objects are mixed in the competition set-up it may be preferable to concentrate on perfection with both types of article in parallel, then to mix the objects for both metal and leather discrimination.

PROBLEMS

Scenting problems are many and varied, although they may manifest themselves with limited diversity. Some dogs seem to forget the reason for going out to the scenting area and meander around without a care in the world. Others will dash out and pick up anything in sight whilst a number seem to be so confused and worried that they are quite incapable of acknowledging the scent they have been given. It is also notable that some dogs are severely chastised for bringing the wrong article back and they are finally left in a sea of confusion.

A number of devious devices are used by some handlers and trainers to try and overcome these problems without giving due consideration to the root cause. Objects can be weighted or pinned to the ground so that the dog cannot bring back the wrong one and, on occasions, these methods do work, but do they get to the source of the problems?

The answer to any of these problems should be reached through an analysis of the cause. Is it basically a retrieving fault? Perhaps there is a hang-up due to a hasty or ill-prepared change from the handler's scent to that of a stranger? Whatever the cause, a return to basic schooling should be considered with the motto of *Success breeds success and failure encourages confusion.*

To continue attending shows where the opportunities of failures are great can only compound a fault. It is not uncommon to find handlers struggling with a particular problem for a year or more after the fault had initially become evident. This is mainly because the handler would not give up a few weeks of competing so that the problem could be cleared up without the pressure of the following week's show.

JUDGING

A judge has full scope to set out his scenting exercise within the confines of the Kennel Club Regulations. The pattern, or lack of pattern, for the objects and articles is his choice, with the location of the decoy objects also being determined by the judge. He does, however, need to pay some attention to detail, especially in Class C where his own scent is being used for scenting the cloth to be retrieved.

The marking of faults is generally carried out within the normal approach applied for all other exercises. To give extra commands or encouragement whilst the dog is actually discriminating would result in the loss of all marks. The same would apply if the dog returned with the wrong article.

A number of judges seem to ignore the fact that some dogs fail to work continuously during the exercise and, therefore, encourage faulty schooling practices. Judges have been seen to give full marks to dogs who meandered round the ring then seemed to stumble on the correct article and yet they would penalize other dogs for a slightly crooked sit after doing a very attentive and workmanlike scent discrimination.

Although the UK Obedience Regulations do not give any guidance in the method of marking, the US Regulations make it very clear that a dog who is inattentive or does not work continuously must receive minor to substantial penalties, depending on the circumstances.

FOR THE DOMESTIC PET

The owner of the domestic pet dog, who has no interest in attaining a competitive standard, will find innumerable party tricks where success can be guaranteed if discrimination is limited to his own scent. Schooling should be based on the Class A and B routines with the enthusiasm of a good retriever. The precision required for competitive work can be ignored with scenting being carried out in a more carefree and relaxed atmosphere.

1. A dog who likes to retrieve your car keys will soon find them if they are placed amongst those of your friends when all the keys have been distributed over the floor.

2. Your handkerchief displayed on the floor with a number of others should not create any difficulties. Your dog's patriotism can be demonstrated by having him return to you with a handkerchief-sized Union Jack, which you have handled and laid out with the flags of other nations.

3. A row of wooden clothes pegs placed on the floor by a friend can have another peg handled by yourself placed in the line-up. The friend can put your article into the line so long as he does not handle it. To carry the peg on a piece of paper is probably the best way of avoiding contamination.

4. To take a playing card from a pack, scent it well and then have it placed on the floor with others well spread out will ensure a hearty sound of applause when your dog returns to you with the chosen card.

5. A favourite game for a number of training clubs when they are giving a demonstration is to have each participant with a piece of white cloth marked distinctly with a letter to make up the name of the club or location of the demonstration. A demonstration for a Gala Day at Broxburn could have a team of eight members, each with a cloth lettered in the correct order so that each dog would return with his handler's

scented cloth to be displayed until the full place name of BROXBURN was evident to the audience.

As these exercises are intended principally for the domestic pet owner and the use of scenting in party tricks there is no harm in taking advantage of dual-scenting when the audience does not realize that you have removed some saliva from the dog's mouth with your finger-tips whilst you were fondling him. Holding the article in the hand will then ensure dual-scenting and a more positive identification of your article.

Dogs enjoy showing off just as much as their owners and this helps to develop a happy companionship.

10

Article Searching

INTRODUCTION

Searching for articles which have been lost or dropped in the undergrowth is one of the most pleasurable pastimes a dog can enjoy. It is another application which involves the use of his olfactory system where he can cast around with his nose near to the ground to seek out any article bearing a human scent. It is a pastime to be enjoyed by the domestic pet, an exercise to be worked at more seriously in the working trials schedule or a practical task in the pursuit of crime detection.

Although this chapter is written around the requirements of the competitive exercise for the British Kennel Club Working Trials schedule, the approach to the schooling of a domestic pet is the same where a dog can be taught to search around for lost keys, a glove or a piece of jewellery which has been dropped by accident. The schooling of a service dog is based on the very same principles.

THE COMPETITION EXERCISE

The competition exercise involves searching for four articles in a piece of ground twenty-five yards square, with a post at each corner to define the area to be worked. The articles are handled and placed by a stranger to the dog and the ground may well be foiled by another person and dog if the judge so desires. The articles may be of any size or composition other than food or glass. The Kennel Club, however, give guidance that the articles should be similar in size to a six-inch nail or a matchbox although these conditions can be varied to suit the nature of the ground. A maximum of five minutes is allowed and a minimum of two articles must be found and returned to the handler to be eligible for a qualification. During this five minute working period the handler is not permitted to move into the search area but is permitted to move round the perimeter to control his dog to the greatest advantage. He is also permitted to talk to, instruct or encourage his dog without penalty.

These conditions are relevant to the full exercise required for the qualifying stakes through Utility Dog (U.D.) to the top Police Dog (P.D.) or Tracker Dog (T.D.) titles. The preliminary stake for the Companion Dog (C.D.) title involves the searching for three articles in a marked area of fifteen yards square. A maximum time limit of four minutes is set and a minimum of two articles must be found.

Schooling should be based on the requirements for the full exercise unless the handler with the smaller dog has no intention of progressing beyond the C.D. Stake. The details which follow are based on requirements for the major exercise. Competitors who wish to concentrate on the C.D. Stake can, however, restrict their working area, also limit the searching time and number of articles to suit the exercise.

DEVELOPING THE CORRECT ATTITUDES
The search exercise can be the downfall of many a dog in working trials. A busy dog working all the time but failing to achieve the success his efforts deserve will find the five minute time limit to be rather short, but to the disinterested dog who is forced to spend the full period in the search area it will seem like eternity.

Many handlers stumble from trials to trials breathing a sigh of relief if the dog manages to bring out two articles, and consider a third one to be a bonus. Unfortunately, some poor searchers qualify because a good track mark can, on occasions, subsidize a poor search and there can be little incentive for some handlers to reconsider their attitude towards the exercise. At the same time, I think it is a pity to waste a good tracking performance because of a poor search.

To become a good, enthusiastic, competitive searcher a dog must be a determined retriever, one who is reluctant to give up when he knows there is something to be found, one who will pick up any reasonable material in most shapes or forms. Any attempt to develop the full routine with a dog who is not a proficient retriever can, at the very least, detract from a competent performance and, at the worst, can result in many more failures than successes.

The groundwork is, therefore, built on keenness to retrieve. With a number of dogs this can be considered as a project in itself, not necessarily for the requirements of a controlled obedience-style retrieve but a free and easy application where the dog is prepared to return immediately and deliver to hand. In fact, a competitive obedience style retrieve is more likely to inhibit a dog and can easily result in a mediocre searching performance. However, the basis for good sound retrieving has already been given in Chapter 5.

The keenness to search can be developed at any time; specific training sessions are not necessary in the early stages and they may in fact inhibit your own approach. Any time you are out for a walk throw a suitably weighted article into the undergrowth or into grass which is long enough to ensure that the dog is more likely to pick up the scent rather than the sight of it. Let him pinpoint the dropping zone with his eyes and watch how his nose takes over when he gets within scenting distance.

If you throw an article into the wind he should locate the scent before he reaches the article, but if you throw with a following wind he must cast beyond the article to determine its location. Schooling for the search exercise can begin when the groundwork has been achieved and a reasonable measure of persistence to find a thrown article.

A dog can only search for the required period, up to five minutes in competition, if he is allowed to develop at his own rate. To ask a dog to continue searching after he has lost the desire can only encourage boredom and resentment with performances deteriorating to predictably low levels. It is, therefore, very important that consideration be given to terminate on success, before the dog reaches his limit of persistence.

The handler's attitude whilst a dog is searching is also important. He must learn to keep quiet whilst the dog is working well, he should be prepared to give a little encouragement when the dog seems to 'wind' an article, he should also show real pleasure when the dog has picked up the article and then genuine appreciation when the article is delivered to hand.

To try and apply strict control or to nag at the dog for any reason whatsoever can only distract him from the job in hand. If his mind has already been distracted, nagging or pressurizing will not meet with the desired long-term result and is likely to ensure that distractions become an excuse for rather than the cause of failures.

DEVELOPING THE ROUTINE

The process to date has been based on scent retrieving where visual acknowledgement of the thrown article has been followed by the dog scenting to pinpoint its exact location. To develop a routine which will ensure that the dog understands what is wanted of him and to maintain his enthusiasm for lengthy periods, a visual approach should be continued until the full exercise has been successfully accomplished.

The excitement of searching and the knowledge that articles have been placed into a specific area are the primary inducements. The finding of articles is essentially the supreme inducement which will become the vehicle of enthusiasm throughout the dog's working life.

To develop the full exercise schooling must be based on the following considerations:

1. Ensure that the dog is quite happy to work at a distance. As the search area is twenty-five yards square, the dog should become accustomed to working at the extreme distance. A dog who insists on working round a handler's feet is quite useless.
2. The dog should have the enthusiasm to return to the search area to find more articles as soon as he has brought one to hand.

Working distance and a widening of the search area will be given the first consideration.

When a dog watches an article being thrown or placed and

is then released for a scent retrieve he will make directly for the dropping zone. Some dogs can visually locate the area to within a couple of feet whilst others seem to have a less accurate sense of visual location. The area of search should be gradually broadened and the first step can be achieved by breaking the dog's continuity of vision after throwing or placing the article. This can be done by turning him round in a circle or walking in front of him immediately before he is released to search for his article. It is amazing how this little ploy can break the accuracy of visual location and, although the dog will go out in the general direction, he will need to make greater use of his nose to identify the actual location of the article.

At the same time the creation of distance between handler and the working area should be developed. Every search should be based on a distance of fifteen to thirty yards from the handler and where possible the dog should be worked into the wind. However, if your dog has difficulty in finding an article, your positioning in relation to the wind and distance become secondary considerations. Rather than direct a dog towards an article it is preferable to be positioned so that the dog can be drawn towards the handler and across the scent of the article.

Drawing a dog onto an article brings out a very important point. To send or direct a dog into an area requires a certain amount of compulsion and each send-out or redirect can be draining enthusiasm from a dog's searching desire, whereas drawing a dog towards you and across an article will not have any adverse effect unless it is carried out in a demanding manner.

Whilst repositioning yourself it is important that you do not draw the dog's attention to your movements. The advantage is lost if your dog comes back to you every time you move and we often see handlers running round the search area with the dog following to heel. This only encourages a dog to watch his handler's every movement and to respond to these movements by returning to him and needing to be sent out again. As already stated, every send-out eventually drains enthusiasm.

Care should also be taken not to inhibit the dog prior to a search, even a most elementary search. When you throw or place an article give your dog freedom at the end of the lead, either by holding the lead or hooking it onto a post, and encourage eager anticipation for the exercise. At this stage a variety of decent sized articles can be used; they will be dual-scented but this is quite acceptable until the full routine has been established.

Multiple article searching can now be developed by applying the principles of both scent retrieving and searching. Take two articles and throw them out together so that they land reasonably close to each other. The dog will visually focus on one and will carry out a scenting retrieve. Encourage him to go out for the second and if need be help him. It is this second article which helps to develop the dog's approach to searching. It is the knowledge that another article is somewhere in the region which induces him to return to the area.

Some dogs catch on very quickly whilst others take some time before they fully appreciate the significance of the second article. It is very important, however, not to develop to a third or fourth article until the two-article routine is well established.

Developing a keenness for the second article ensures a quick return with the first and the desire to get back out there to search. A continuation of this procedure with three articles, then with four and possibly five articles, and with the dog working at a good distance will establish the basic pattern required for a good search.

The issuing of commands should be avoided at all times and gentle encouragement should be the order of the day. I find it helpful to talk my dog into a state of mind where he expects a search and this approach sets the pattern for the dog when he has not witnessed the placing of search articles. When I release my dog to search it is with an encouraging question, 'Are you going to find it, son?' As there can be no penalties for extra commands, there is never any need to shorten the phrase although the shortened 'Find it, son' is used as required as encouragement during the period of searching.

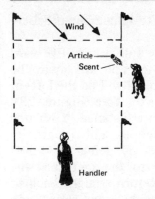

Fig. 22 Effect of wind on search exercise.

DEVELOPING THE SEARCH

In developing the routine the area for searching has not been purposely foiled. This has made it easier to locate the articles and witnessing them being thrown has been sufficient to take the dog into the correct area.

As the dog has always been released to go straight out in front of the handler he anticipates and responds by going out in the general direction required. The area for searching should now be foiled so that the dog can associate the odours of crushed vegetation, the scent of humans and possibly a dog, with the searching area and can eventually restrict his own movements to within the invisible perimeter of the scented area.

The process of foiling a piece of ground is simply to walk back and forth to cause additional odours and scents.

If the articles are always to be found within a foiled area, or at least an area bounded by the human scent left behind by the search steward when he placed the four corner marker posts, the dog will eventually learn to spend his time working within the area of scent. Remember that wind will carry the scent beyond the boundary markers and a dog should not be discouraged from using that scent to locate an article (see Figure 22).

The use of the four corner posts to mark the search area is intended to be for the benefit of the handler, the steward and the judge in competition and should not be considered as a guide to the dog. Without the corner posts or the use of some natural markers it would be difficult to remember precisely where the articles have been located.

At each working session set out the full twenty-five yard search area and foil one quarter only. As you will always be working into the wind the area to be foiled will be the left- or right-handed quarter furthest from you (see Figure 23).

It is essential to keep working from a distance. Your dog can be tied to a fence or held by somebody and the articles can also be dropped whilst the area is being foiled. If necessary draw your dog's attention to the fact that the articles are dropped for his benefit. Return straight back to your dog; the single scent path caused by your return will probably help to ensure that your dog makes straight for the foiled area when released.

During the period of searching do not enter the marked area unless you have decided to terminate by helping to finish on an article.

At each session alternate between the left- and right-hand quarter until you feel your dog is ready to tackle the full back-half of the marked area. Do not be in any hurry to develop into the full area; it can take quite some time to develop the keenness to maintain a working distance. Even when the full working area has been developed, I have generally found it beneficial to foil the back-half of the

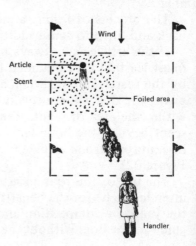

Fig. 23 Achieving a working distance
for the search exercise.

marked area on two out of three searches until the dog is well-experienced, and periods of re-education may necessitate a return to this technique.

The time taken to develop the pattern of searching is spread over quite a period and this allows the starting routine to become firmly established whilst the dog is watching the articles being placed into the search area.

Bringing a dog to a marked out search area with a post in each corner may now be sufficient to stimulate the desire to search even without seeing the articles being placed. Although some dogs may not respond quite so readily, it can be helpful to break in the blind search gradually. Let the dog see the articles being placed in the area then take him for a short walk to allow a few minutes to elapse before releasing him to search. When your dog is prepared to accept a ten minute delay without drawing on his enthusiasm he is probably ready for a completely blind search.

ARTICLES AND SCENTS
Success in schooling depends to a great extent on the articles which are used, the amount of scent on them and the nature of that scent. As the principle of progress is again based on 'Success breeds success and failure encourages confusion', the size and scenting of articles contributes to the end result.

Initially good sized articles, which are easily picked up, must help to give a dog confidence. The type of article shown in Figure 10 for tracking (see page 94) can also be used for searching.

Dual-scenting can be the basis for building up a keenness to search and can also be used intermittently to help maintain a vigorous approach to searching.

The introduction of other people's scents can be helped by having fun retrieves with articles thrown by friends, to encourage a dog to accept the presence of their scent on articles in the search. This introduction of other people's scented articles into the search area should again be carried out in full view of the dog, with the assistant taking the dog's attention. Progress to blind searches should only be made when the dog responds accordingly.

Although these searches may be blind to the dog the handler should know precisely where the articles have been placed until he has full confidence in his dog. A dog who indicates an article then fails to pick it up is likely to develop the habit of ignoring the articles he would prefer not to know. If the handler does not know where the articles have been placed he will not know whether the dog is investigating one or not.

Acknowledging an article's presence but failing to bring it back must be countered immediately by the handler moving up to the article and giving his dog encouragement and close moral support so that he will pick up the article. It is possible that even with moral support a dog may refuse to pick up an article. This is the time to terminate the search and concentrate on fun retrieves with the article in question.

To let him ignore the article and continue the search is likely to introduce an undesirable attitude towards certain articles or scents. To make him pick it up, especially from a distance, is likely to inhibit future searches, but to make a retrieving game of it will certainly ensure that the article or scent is more acceptable in the future.

A continuation of single- and dual-scenting can be used along with a variation in size or type of article in the search area. One or two articles bearing the dog's scent as well as the assistant's and the rest with the assistant's scent only can help to give a dog an encouraging start to a search. As most dogs become discouraged through failures or a long time between the finding of each article, a few searches for three or four poorly-scented articles can do more harm than good.

It is not necessary to make every search an easy one, but too many frustrating searches will soon demoralize the dog. Where possible finish each search on success, even if your assistant has to drop another article surreptitiously to ensure a find.

CONTROL

A dog should require the minimum of control whilst he is searching. He may need to be drawn into a section of the search area which has not been fully investigated, or he may

spend unwarranted effort searching outside the marked area
and again may need to be drawn back into the correct area
for searching. It must be remembered, however, that articles
may have been deposited at the base of a marker post or right
on the perimeter of the search area and that markers show
only the boundary for articles, not necessarily the absolute
limit of the area to be worked.

A handler should be prepared to re-position himself at any
time before venturing to draw his dog into a selected area.
Talking to a dog whilst he is working can be an irritating
distraction and nagging plays no part in maintaining or
regenerating an enthusiastic performance.

A handler needs to be absolutely vigilant whilst his dog is
working and any indication of article recognition may require
that little word of encouragement to convince the dog that
he should stop and investigate. Many an important article is
lost because that slight indication from the dog has gone
unnoticed.

During a search the dog is expected to give his full concentration – he is also entitled to expect the same consideration
from his partner.

JUDGING
The judging of any exercise is a two-part business and the
search is no exception. It consists of:

1. Setting an exercise which will test the dog's ability to
   locate and retrieve acceptable articles.
2. Assessing each individual performance against the
   requirements of the schedule.

The selection of articles will depend to some extent on the
type of ground which has been made available. If the undergrowth is very heavy a very small article can become buried
and the surrounding odours from crushed vegetation may
well mask the minimal amount of scent from the article; on
the other hand, short grass can leave many an article in full
view of the dog and handler.

Articles made from porous materials can absorb a fair
amount of human scent and are popular with any handler.

Most metals, although they lack porosity, seem to be good scent carriers but some plastics give reason for concern. A greater in-depth study would be required with a specialist's knowledge of plastics to comment further on this subject.

Some search stewards are guilty of taking articles out of the container and immediately depositing them in the search area without giving the articles a reasonable opportunity to collect sufficient scent. It has even been known for a steward to take an article out of a plastic bag with finger and thumb and immediately drop it in the search area, move round to another spot and do likewise with the next. It is the judge's responsibility to ensure that his steward understands his requirements in scenting articles.

A judge may have various purposes in mind when he selects his articles. There may be one large or awkward article to test a dog's retrieving versatility, or there could be an article which looks like rubbish left around as litter, such as a milk bottle top or a piece of twig. More than once I have seen a competitor throw such an article away thinking it was a piece of rubbish.

The positioning of articles in the search area and the relationship to wind direction are other factors worthy of consideration. The judge obviously requires each article to be inconspicuous to both canine and human eye and articles placed near the edge of the area should blend into the background; articles placed nearer the centre are less likely to be visible to the handler.

Many handlers expect to find an article within each quarter of the area and some judges will put two or three into one particular sector to assess the hander's mental approach to the exercise. For the same reason an article may be placed on the edge or in a corner of the marked area. All these practices are quite legitimate and help to show the amount of thought behind a handler's reasoning during the exercise.

The marking of an individual performance must be considered against the requirements of the schedule; comparison with that of other partnerships in the competition is of secondary consideration.

Each article is valued at seven marks and their return is

usually rewarded with full marks for each. A badly chewed or damaged article can result in a reduction in marks for the article in question. Another seven marks are allocated for 'Control' and 'Style'. I sometimes think that this should be reworded as 'Style with appropriate measure of Control'.

Style is a difficult matter to describe as this varies from one partnership to another and is probably based on the development of the dog's natural ability. A judge should not demand or expect a particular style of work from a dog or even a style of control from a handler to the job in hand.

Control is a completely different factor: excessive control can have a very inhibiting effect and control at the wrong time can be disastrous. How often have we seen a dog give a very clear indication of an article only to find that the handler has ignored it and redirected the dog into another sector of the area. On the other hand dogs have been left to run around with little thought of searching whilst the handler stands passively by like a disinterested onlooker.

A handler may need to move round the perimeter of the search area to apply the correct measure of control and there are times when he may have to use the windward side of the area. Many judges will penalize a competitor out of hand because the handler has allowed his scent to be blown into the search area, thereby making the exercise more difficult for the dog. This may well be so, but if a dog fails to return with an article because of this movement he fails to earn the seven marks for the article and receives a double penalty. If such a purposeful movement results in finding an article the measure was successful and should warrant the judge's appreciation.

Some partnerships warrant a poor 'Style and Control' mark even with the return of all four articles, but others, which have executed an admirable performance, may well have had limited success and deserve every mark the judge can honestly award.

11

Quartering for a Hidden Person

INTRODUCTION

To have a dog quarter a piece of ground or a building is to have him searching for someone, either a missing person or a criminal in hiding. The person may be hidden in a wood, in a ditch, behind a rock or in some obscure and unexpected location in a building. A properly trained dog, however, is expected to cover the ground to the left, to the right and ahead of his handler until he finds some indication of that person's presence. One or all of his three senses can become operative to acknowledge the presence of the person in question and in practice any of these senses can determine the true location. These senses are SIGHT, SOUND and SCENT.

Although sight and sound will be fully utilized during the initial period of schooling, scenting is the principal sense which will locate the majority of hidden persons and the objective is to bring the principle of wind scenting to the fore where the body scent of the hidden person is borne by currents of air so that it can be detected by the dog's olfactory system.

Quartering is a practical application of wind scenting used extensively by the police, security services and the armed forces. Used professionally a dog should be able to detect, locate and give voice when he finds a missing person. This person may be lying asleep or injured, or he could be a hardened criminal who would be prepared to go to any length to make his escape. Quartering is also an exercise which is applied within the P.D. Stake schedule in working trials and should be worked within the requirements of the practical police dog.

As already stated, the objectives can be to find an innocent missing person or a hardened criminal and a fully trained dog must react in a manner to suit the circumstances. In the case of an innocent person the dog should give voice and let his handler know of the location but he should show no sign of aggression which could cause alarm to an innocent party, as this could be a child or an elderly person who is already in a distressed condition. On the other hand it could be a suspected criminal to be located and the dog would have to be extremely watchful and be prepared to defend himself or to prevent the suspect from escaping until his handler is available to take control of the situation.

To prepare a dog for the latter he would be introduced to the fundamental principles of attack training and it is not my intention to describe this field of study. Agitation and the development of attack training is a specialized subject which requires the assistance of highly experienced and capable assistants: with help of that calibre at hand who needs a book? Attack training can be a dangerous subject if it is not properly executed and I would not like to feel responsible through my writing for any misdirected efforts.

Schooling to quarter and the reaction on finding an innocent person may not be as dramatic or exciting as developing the process through agitation, and some dogs can lack the real incentive to go out and find without having some form of attack training, but the principle put forward is very effective in training this exercise. This approach will allow a greater number of handlers to achieve the full development of quartering, locating and giving voice without the worry of attack training. The final element of aggression can be developed at a subsequent stage with experienced assistants if it becomes a desirable feature of the complete exercise.

The quartering exercise is only one part of the full P.D. schedule where attack and defence training is essential. This, of course, limits the number and type of participants to within the field of working trials but many a household pet would enjoy a less formal approach which could add a new dimension to his life with the children.

The full exercise can be broken down into three components:

1. Inducing the dog to speak when required.
2. Inducing him to find a hidden person and to respond by giving voice.
3. Teaching him to quarter the ground or to search a building until the hidden person is found.

INDUCEMENT TO SPEAK

Giving voice is a very natural activity for a dog but achieving this action when we want it can be a different story. Although some dogs need little inducement a great deal of patience is required to achieve a satisfactory response from many others.

A dog can be encouraged to continue speaking when he starts of his own volition or he can be induced by creating a situation where he will want to give voice. The former condition can make the task very simple but a quieter dog may pose quite a problem. We cannot command, instruct or ask a quieter dog to speak but should always try to find a more natural situation which will result in an active response.

If your dog gives voice when some stranger comes in the front gate or knocks at the door, encourage him. If he gives voice when you tease him a little with a titbit or his dinner, again encourage him. If he barks with excitement because you have his ball or some squeaky toy, let him know how clever he is. You may wish to tie him to a fence whilst you have an excited game with the children, or even your other dog, and this may induce him to give voice. The main point is to encourage him whilst he is barking through enticement, rather than trying to encourage him without the inducement which suits his character. One form of inducement can be highly successful with one dog but fail to have any effect on another.

For the purpose of inducing the speak the reward of a thrown ball or his favourite squeaky toy would be most appropriate and should help to develop the most suitable response. Perhaps I should warn you about the dangers of using a ball which is small enough to stick in a dog's throat, or even be swallowed. I have witnessed the distress of one dog with a ball firmly lodged in his throat and the anguish of the owners as we worked to remove it, so do make sure the ball is big enough to avoid this danger.

The use of a ball is one form of stimulus which can be used by one person or another and one should bear in mind that the dog is finally expected to give voice without the direct influence of his handler. Although food can be used with a pet dog to stimulate activity, the professional or trials dog handler must consider the refusal of food from other people as part of the dog's training. However, a ball or some other suitable article held in the hand can be used as a signal to give voice. With some dogs an empty clenched fist is an adequate signal.

The whole process is based on exaggerated signals being gradually replaced by diminishing indications until the dog responds to the situation rather than a signal. If your dog can be taught to respond to a hand movement with a ball in view especially with the hand held high and with a vigorous movement, the arm can eventually be dropped with a slight twist of the wrist to show the ball.

The quick, but minor, movements can help a dog to give voice when he finds a hidden person during training and the association of finding and speaking which is immediately followed by a fun retrieve can keep a dog very attentive to the presence of the hidden person until the handler arrives on the scene.

As friends or members of the family can be used as hidden persons they can all help with the initial speak training if this suits the dog, or they can be introduced with the inducive article when you have perfected this element of the exercise yourself.

The second stage, that of going out to find the hidden person, should not be considered until at least one assistant can be depended on to have the dog giving voice at will. The development of an instant speak on finding the assistant without minor movements as an inducement can become part of the follow-up training for the quarter and seek out.

INDUCEMENT TO SEEK OUT

The initial purpose which should now be instilled into the dog's mind is to go out to a known hiding place, find the assistant who is acting as the missing person and speak so that he can get his ball.

With your dog on the lead, have the assistant tease him with the ball just sufficiently to get him excited and to want it. The assistant can then run off with the ball and hide behind a tree, in a ditch or round the corner of a building – a distance of twenty to fifty yards should be sufficient. Your dog should be encouraged to watch and should be desperate to follow. As soon as the assistant is out of sight let your dog take you to the hiding place or release him so that you can follow at your own pace.

You should not be required to play any further part in the proceedings as the assistant is now in full control and he will create any inducement necessary to have your dog give voice. If the previous training has been correctly carried out the inducement should result in an immediate response, three to five seconds of giving voice should be sufficient; then the dog should be fully rewarded by fun and games with his ball.

One to three similar seek outs in one session are probably quite sufficient and it is important that your dog is full of enthusiasm on each occasion. With some dogs one seek out is quite sufficient whilst others can enjoy more frequent trials in each session.

The dog is not taught by command but each time he is released a phrase should be used which will eventually trigger off the seek out. I usually use the trigger phrase of 'Where is he?' to focus the dog's attention on the proceedings. Initially, of course, he is watching the assistant go out of sight and the expression is just fixing it in his mind for the day he does not see the assistant disappear from view. 'Where is he?' is usually followed by 'Go and get him' as the dog is released.

If your inducement is strong enough, your dog will soon respond by giving voice as soon as he finds the assistant or when the assistant gives a very minor movement of the hand to indicate the presence of the ball.

A variety of hiding places can be used and with each one your dog should initially see the assistant going out of sight. A trial can then be made by having the assistant going out of sight before your dog is brought to the scene. Wind scenting now becomes an important feature of the exercise and your dog should be brought to the area in a direction which will give him the opportunity of picking up the body scent of the assistant as it drifts through the air. It may be advisable to have your dog indicate the presence of the assistant via his body scent in the air before releasing him for the first few trials. Thereafter, canine confidence, through success, can dictate the working distances.

As the assistant is still the main controlling influence he should be watching the release of your dog and any indecision should immediately be countered by the assistant drawing attention to himself, either by noise or coming into sight, or both, but for just sufficient time to achieve his objective.

As your dog gains experience and confidence the period for giving voice can be extended until your dog's attention automatically remains with the assistant until the handler arrives on the scene.

The initial inducement should never be forgotten and the dog must be given the reward which will induce him to go out with confidence and keenness the next time he is asked.

This stage of training can be considered as satisfactory when the dog is prepared to go to an obvious hiding place which has not been used before and immediately give voice on finding the hidden person.

TO QUARTER IN THE OPEN

The dog knows from his earlier experience that a landmark, be it a tree, a bush, a telegraph pole, a wall or a building, may well conceal a person in hiding, but the person could also be lying on the ground or in a ditch. The pattern for quartering should, therefore, be developed to cover the unseen as well as the obvious hiding place.

Quartering is very much an activity of having your dog visually focus in the direction you wish to send him but on moving out he should be prepared to deviate if an airborne scent indicates the presence of a person out of his direct line of movement. His olfactory system will then act as a homing device which will lead your dog directly to his objective.

Select a field or other suitable area with points of cover; most should be suitable for an assistant to stand or crouch behind, others can be at ground level where a person can remain out of sight until your dog is right on top of him.

The starting point and the handler's base line should be right up the centre of the area from one end to the other. This can be seen as a line X–Y in Figure 24. Two hiding places will initially be required, one to the right and the other to the left and shown as hides A and B in Figure 24. Whilst you are at the end of the field with your dog have the assistant walk round the edge and disappear behind A; you do not wish to have a scent path between yourself and the hide. The dog has been watching and he knows what is coming; this is a simple seek out from a sighting. Now release your dog to find the assistant and then to give voice. As soon as he starts speaking go and join your dog to finish the element with a fun retrieve.

Walk back round the field with your dog and the assistant, then take the dog out of sight as the assistant returns round the field and conceals himself again behind hide A. When you have returned and taken up your stance as before, release your dog with the trigger phrase 'Where is he?' Any indecision should bring an immediate reaction from the assistant to draw attention to himself, but I doubt if this will be necessary.

On completion of this element and if you are satisfied with your dog's response, have the assistant move round the edge of the field to hide B, but with this new hide make sure your dog is well out of sight as you want him to believe that hide A is still occupied. Return to point X with your dog and release him in the direction of hide A with the usual encouragement. His quartering to the right will be fruitless and as soon as he has discovered the hide to be empty have the assistant come into view and shout to draw attention to himself. Immediately your dog reacts, the assistant should hide again so that the element can be completed in the normal manner. This should be sufficient for one session.

During the next training session repeat the procedure, but start with hide B and finish with hide A. The training sessions should be repeated until your dog is prepared to work the two hides in any order without knowing which will be occupied.

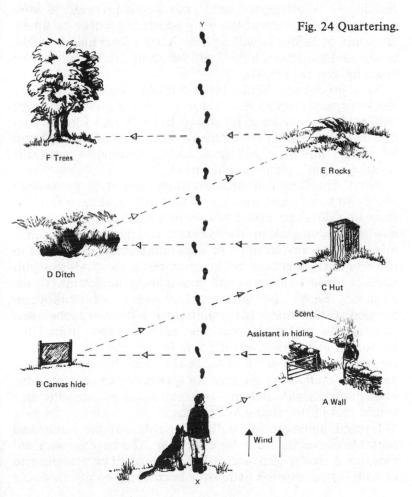

Fig. 24 Quartering.

Line X–Y in Figure 24 should be maintained as the handler's base line during this and the more advanced stages and he should not leave this line until the dog has located the assistant and given voice. Remember the assistant is in full control after you release your dog and your role is now passive until the hidden assistant has been located.

Location C can now be added to the active hides with your dog quartering to hide A and hide B, then the assistant draws your dog's attention to his new hide. The fourth hide D should not be attempted until your dog is prepared to work each active hide without knowing which one will be occupied. On some occasions it will be hide A, on others hide B will be in use and sometimes hide C will be occupied. Keep your dog guessing, but enthusiastic.

This procedure should be developed until your dog can work his way through half a dozen hides. A change of venue will probably require a return to hides A and B until your dog becomes familiar with his new surroundings. Each change of venue, however, will give added experience until the routine is firmly planted in his mind.

Wind direction can be important and it is your dog's ability to wind scent which results in him making a find. To train in a direction which results in a head or cross wind can have your dog pick up the scent of an assistant earlier than intended and any attempt to make him quarter the hides in the opposite direction could only result in confusion; his mind is tuned to locating and highlighting the position of the assistant. Figure 24 shows the direction of working in relation to the wind when training with three or more hides.

It is also preferable that the assistant moves round the perimeter of the field when going from one hide to another to avoid leaving a scent path behind him, but on the other hand you could have the area for quartering so contaminated with human scent that the assistant walking across the area would make little, if any, difference.

Natural hides are generally advisable but the occasional portable canvas hide can have its value. To have an assistant hide up a tree is also useful but he must draw attention to himself if your dog is a little slow in catching on.

TO SEARCH A BUILDING

Assuming that the element of giving voice has been perfected and your dog responds to an assistant with a ball, the search of a building can be started in a similar manner to that of quartering in the open. Although your dog responds to an assistant in the open he may not be so ready to give voice whilst in a building, so make sure he will give voice where and when required before beginning indoor work.

Farm buildings are an ideal site; derelict warehouses, factories or such like where there are plenty of places to hide are also suitable for searching.

Have an assistant go and hide at a prearranged spot behind a door, a piece of machinery, in a cupboard or some such place. As you bring your dog to the vicinity of the hiding place have the assistant make his presence known, by sight, sound or both. Again remember that the assistant is in control of the situation and the reward of a thrown ball or some such article should continue to be the inducement to find the assistant.

Your dog now knows the hiding place and will remember it for the second trial. Take him out of sight again, then release him with the trigger phrase 'Where is he?' It is now more difficult for the assistant to assess the dog's reaction, as in the open he could watch your dog's movements from his hiding place but now he must judge your dog's reaction and help when necessary with a cough, a scuffle of feet or the movement of a door to help draw his attention.

Scenting the assistant in a building can be much more difficult than wind scenting in the open as the scent in a building tends to become trapped; a room may well be filled with human scent but the hiding place may go undetected until the dog becomes experienced.

I remember an assistant who hid in a wooden trunk and the relatively inexperienced dog who was being trained kept passing this trunk. It was only the sound of movement inside which finally drew his attention to this hiding place.

Two hiding places can now be used in different areas of the building or even two rooms of a derelict house. Follow your dog to the one which was already in use and when he finds it to be vacant indicate the direction to the second hide. Your directing will be heard by the assistant and he can draw attention to his new hiding place.

Success can bring in a third hide and the build-up should be generated in the same manner as out door quartering. A new venue means starting again until experience and enthusiasm ensure success when breaking fresh ground.

The full value of experience is shown by your dog's ability to cope with more difficult or unusual situations. Have him use his eyes and ears as well as his nose as the slightest sound or movement can help to locate a hidden person. A man hiding in the rafters will be missed by a novice, but not by a properly trained dog.

One police dog handler, who was acting as a wanted person, sat quite openly on a window-sill in a derelict farm house. He was sitting reading a newspaper when the dog came in, nosed round the likely place, ignored the obvious and went out to declare the room as clear. There was a lesson to be learned and one dog handler certainly taught the other.

CONTROL

Quartering to seek out a hidden person is another exercise where the element of control is most evident when it is lacking and the handler has to keep shouting commands to try and direct his dog to the hide in question or his dog just ignores him and goes his own way.

The handler's function should be a simple one, that of directing his dog from one hide to another. He will then take charge of events when the person has been found.

The assistant who is acting as the missing person is the key to a well-trained dog and the handler is but a junior partner.

JUDGING

Setting out an exercise in competition requires a fair amount of advance planning with the probability of modifications on the day to cater for any unexpected situations.

The direction of the wind is important if a reasonable amount of quartering is to be carried out before the hidden person is to be found. Natural hides and the availability of artificial hides can help make the exercise a spectacular event as well as a practical one. The positions of spectators and the assurance that nobody can stray into the area which is to be worked is also very important.

Judging each dog and the subsequent marking is very much in the eye of the beholder but the quality of performance can be based on two factors:

1. The dog's ability to work on his own with the handler redirecting only when one hide has been cleared as empty, and the dog's immediate response to his handler's requirements.
2. The dog's reaction on finding the hidden person with the ability to give voice and remain with his find.

These factors are not easy to achieve, they require a great deal of work, patience and planning during the period of training.

Postscript

Canine scenting is a fascinating subject and I know no other aspect of dog training which carries such a veil of mystery. We all have our own theories on scents but only the dog knows what he is about and what he can smell. He probably does not know what urge drives him to use his gift in a manner which pleases us, but without that urge or inherited instinct we cannot enjoy the applications described in this book.

I hope that my writings have helped the uninitiated to discover some pleasures of canine scenting and I hope also that dog owners already involved in working trials or obedience competition will have been stimulated into a fresh line of thinking which may eventually reveal more of the scenting mysteries which have puzzled dog trainers for many years.

Kennel Club Working Trials Regulations (S1)
8th November, 1977
(Reproduced by kind permission of the Kennel Club)

1. Management of Working Trials — The management of a Working Trial shall be entrusted to a Working Trial Manager who shall be responsible for ensuring that the regulations are observed but he may not interfere with the Judges' decisions which shall be final.

The Working Trial Manager, appointed by the Committee of the Society holding the Trial, shall decide upon any matter not related to judging and not provided for in the Kennel Club Rules and Regulations for Working Trials and Obedience Classes and may call upon the Judge or Judges to assist with the decision which shall be final. The Working Trial Manager may not compete at the Trial and should be present throughout.

2. Judges — When a Judge, from ill-health or any other unexpected cause, is prevented from attending or finishing a meeting, the Working Trial Manager once the Trial has commenced shall have the power of deciding what action is to be taken.

3. Schedule — A Society holding a Working Trial must issue a schedule which is to be treated as a contract between the Society and the public and neither party is permitted to make any modification before the date of the Trial, except by permission of the Kennel Club, such alterations to be advertised in suitable publications where possible.

The schedule must contain:—

(a) The date and place of the Working Trial.

(b) The latest date for applying for entry at the Trial. A separate official entry form which must be an exact copy of the wording of the specimen entry form issued by the Kennel Club.

(c) The amounts of entry fees and any prize money.

(d) The conditions of the draw for the order of running.

(e) The conditions and qualifications for making entries and for intimating acceptance or refusal of entries.

(f) An announcement that the Working Trial is held under Kennel Club Working Trials Rules and Regulations with such exceptions and conditions as the Committee of the Society may decide. Such exceptions and conditions must have received the approval of the General Committee of the Kennel Club prior to publication of the schedule.

(g)   The definition of each Stake, together with the qualification or limitations for entry in that Stake.

(h)   The names of Judges. An announcement that if the entries in the Companion Dog Stake exceed 30, a Judge may be appointed to judge the Elementary Search and the competitors notified accordingly.

4.   Assessing Weather Conditions — The Working Trial Manager and the Judges should assess the weather conditions and should they consider the weather unfit for holding the Trials the commencement may be postponed until such time as is considered necessary for the Trials to be abandoned and the entry fees returned.

5.   Handling of Dogs by Owner or his Deputy — An owner or handler may handle the dog, but it must be one or the other; and once the dogs have commenced work an owner must not interfere with his dog if he has deputed another person to handle it.

6.   Certification by Judge(s) — The Judge(s) shall certify on a form provided by the Kennel Club that in their opinion the Stake was held in accordance with the Schedule and Kennel Club Rules and Regulations.

7.   Disqualification of Dogs — A dog shall be disqualified by the Judges and removed from the ground if in their opinion it is:

(a)   Unfit to compete by reason of sexual causes.

(b)   Suffering from any infectious or contagious disease.

(c)   Interfering with the safety or chance of winning of an opponent.

(d)   Of such temperament or is so much out of hand as to be a danger to the safety of any person or other animal.

(e)   Likely to cause cruelty to the dog if it continues in the Trial.

If a dog competes which has been exposed to the risk of any contagious or infectious disease during the period of six weeks prior to the Working Trial and/or if any dog shall be proved to be suffering at a Working Trial from any contagious or infectious disease, the owner thereof shall be liable to be dealt with under Rule 9 of the Kennel Club Rules for Working Trials and Obedience Classes.

8.   Certificates — The Judge or Judges shall give certificates at a Championship Working Trial P.D. (Police Dog), T.D. (Tracking Dog), W.D. (Working Dog), U.D. (Utility Dog), and C.D. Companion Dog) Stake to those dogs which have obtained 70% or more marks in each group of exercises in the Stake entered (provided that the dog has complied with any additional requirements for that Stake). The added qualification 'Excellent' shall be awarded should the dog also obtain 80% or more marks of the total for the Stake.

Societies may issue these Qualification Certificates in Championship Stakes to their own design, subject to the approval of the Kennel Club but they must contain the name and breed of the dog, the name of the owner, the title of the Society and date of the Trials, the qualification and marks awarded and the signature of the Judge and Working Trial Manager.

The Judge or Judges at Open Working Trials run to these schedules shall give Certificates of Merit for those dogs whose marks would have gained them a qualification 'Excellent' at a Championship Working Trial, provided that the Certificate contains the following words: 'This Certificate does not entitle the dog named thereon to any qualification recognised by the Kennel Club except entry in appropriate Stakes at Championship Working Trials'. Such Certificates of Merit must contain the name and breed of the dog, the name of the owner, the title of the Society and date of the Trial, the Stake and the marks awarded (without reference to any qualification) and the signature of the Judge(s) and Working Trial Manager.

9. Prizes — The winner of the Stake shall be the dog that has qualified with 70% or more marks in each group of the Stake and has obtained most marks. No dog that has not so qualified shall be placed in the prize list above a qualified dog. If no dog has qualified the dog with the highest number of marks may be awarded the prize. The Judges are also empowered and instructed to withhold any prize or prizes if in their opinion the dogs competing do not show sufficient merit. Nothing in this Regulation shall apply to the award of 'Special' prizes.

10. Penalties for impugning the decisions of the Judges — If anyone taking part in the Trials openly impugns the decision of the Judge or Judges, he is liable to be dealt with by the Committee under Rules 9 or 10 of the Kennel Club Rules for Working Trials and Obedience Classes.

11. Order of Running — The order of running tracks shall be determined by a draw and competitors notified accordingly prior to the day of the Trial.

12. Disqualification for Absence — The Working Trial Manager shall announce the specific time at which a dog or group of dogs may be called for any exercise or group of exercises. Each dog must be brought up at its proper time and in its proper turn without delay. If occasion demands the times and order may be changed at the discretion of the Working Trial Manager with the approval of the Judge or Judges, provided that no hardship is thereby caused to any competitor. If absent when called, the dog shall be liable to be disqualified by the Judge or Judges.

13. Method of Working — The Judge or Judges in consultation with the Working Trial Manager may arrange for dogs to be working singly or together in any numbers. All dogs entered in a Stake shall be tested as far as possible under similar conditions.

14. Regulations Regarding Handling
(a) A person handling a dog may speak, whistle or work it by hand signals as he wishes, but he can be called to order by the Judge or Judges for making unnecessary noise, and if he persists in doing so the Judge or Judges can disqualify the dog.
(b) No person shall carry out punitive correction or harsh handling of a dog.

15.   Awards — All awards made by the Judge or Judges at a Working Trial shall be in accordance with the agreed scale of points approved by the General Committee of the Kennel Club. Equal awards for any of the prizes offered at a Working Trial are prohibited.

16.   Notification of Awards — The Secretary of a Working Trial shall send (within 7 days of the Trial) the Judges' certification and two marked catalogues to the Kennel Club indicating the prize winners and those dogs to which the Judges have awarded Certificates.

17.   Entry Forms — Entry Forms must be in accordance with the approved form which must be issued by the Secretary of the Working Trial, and all entries must be made thereon and not otherwise, and entirely in ink; only one person shall enter on one form. All such entry forms must be preserved by the Committee of a Working Trial meeting for at least twelve months from the last day of the Trial.

18.   Refusal of Entries — The Committee of any Meeting may reserve to themselves the right of refusing any entries on reasonable grounds.

19.   Objections to Dogs — An objection to a dog must be made to the Secretary in writing at any time within twenty-one days of the last day of the meeting upon the objector lodging with the Secretary the sum of £5.00. The deposit may be returned after the General Committee of the Kennel Club has considered the objection. Should any objection be made other than under Regulation 7(a) to 7(e) the dog should be allowed to compete and a full report made to the Kennel Club.

When an objection is lodged the Secretary of the Society must send to the Kennel Club: —

(a)   A copy of the objection.

(b)   The name and address of the objector.

(c)   The name and address of the owner of the dog.

(d)   All relevant evidence.

The objection will then be dealt with by the General Committee of the Kennel Club whose decision shall be final.

No objection shall be invalidated solely on the grounds that it was incorrectly lodged.

If the dog objected to be disqualified, the prize to which it would otherwise have been entitled shall be forfeited, and the dog or dogs next in order of merit shall move up and take the prize or prizes.

No spectator, not being the owner of a dog competing, or his accredited representative has the right to lodge any objection to a dog or to any action taken at the meeting unless he be a member of the Committee of the Society or of the General Committee of the Kennel Club or a Steward. Any objection so lodged will be disregarded.

20.   Withdrawal of dogs from Competition — No dog entered for competition and actually at the meeting, may be withdrawn from competition without notice to the Working Trials Manager. No dog shall compulsorily be withdrawn from a Stake by reason of the fact that it has obtained less than 70% of the marks in any one group.

21. Failure to Participate in Any Exercise – Failure to participate in any exercise in a group in any Stake shall result in failure to qualify in that group.

22. The Working Trials and Obedience Committee shall issue an Appendix to the Schedule of Exercises and Points, "Description of Exercises and Guidance for Judges and Competitors at Working Trials", which they may from time to time alter and in respect of which notice shall be given in the Kennel Gazette.

23. Working Trials for Bloodhounds shall be exempt from Working Trial Regulations 8, 9, 14(a), 15 and 21 and the Definitions of Stakes and Schedule of Exercises and Points. Until further notice the schedule of each Bloodhound Working Trial shall be submitted to the Kennel Club for approval before publication, in accordance with the provision of Rule 3 of the Kennel Club Rules for Working Trials and Obedience Classes.

Definitions of Stakes

When entering for Championship or Open Working Trials, wins at Members Working Trials will not count.

No dog entered in P.D. or T.D. Stakes shall be eligible to enter in any other Stake at the meeting.

All Police dogs shall be considered qualified for entry in W.D. Championship Stakes if they hold the Regional Police Dog qualification "Excellent", provided that such entries are countersigned by the Senior Police Officer I/C when such entries are made. Dogs holding this qualification are not eligible for entry in C.D. or U.D. Open or Championship Stakes, nor in W.D. Open Stakes.

No Working Trial Stake shall be limited to less than 30 dogs. If a limit is imposed on entries in any Stake, it shall be carried out by ballot after the date of closing of entries. Championship T.D. or P.D. Stakes shall not be limited by numbers in any way.

Open Working Trial

Companion Dog (C.D.) Stake – For dogs which have not qualified C.D. Ex or U.D. Ex or won three or more first prizes in C.D. or any prize in U.D. Stakes, W.D. Stakes, P.D. or T.D. Stakes at Open or Championship Working Trials.

Utility Dog (U.D.) Stake – For dogs which have not been awarded a Certificate of Merit in U.D., W.D., P.D. or T.D. Stakes.

Working Dog (W.D.) Stake – For dogs which have been awarded a Certificate of Merit in U.D. Stakes but not in W.D., P.D. or T.D. Stakes.

Tracking Dog (T.D.) Stake – For dogs which have been awarded a Certificate of Merit in W.D. Stakes but not in T.D. Stakes.

Police Dog (P.D.) Stake – For dogs which have been awarded a Certificate of Merit in W.D. Stakes.

Championship Working Trial
Companion Dog (C.D.) Stake — For dogs which have not won three or more first prizes in C.D. Stakes or any prize in any other Stake at Championship Working Trials.

Utility Dog (U.D.) Stake — For dogs which have won a Certificate of Merit in an Open U.D. Stake. A dog is not eligible for entry in this Stake if it has been entered in the W.D. Stake on the same day.

Working Dog (W.D.) Stake — For dogs which have qualified U.D. Ex and have won a Certificate of Merit in Open W.D. Stakes.

Tracking Dog (T.D.) Stake — For dogs which have qualified W.D. Ex and have won a Certificate of Merit in Open T.D. Stakes.

Police Dog (P.D.) Stake — For dogs which have qualified W.D. Ex.

Members Working Trial
This is restricted to the members of the Society holding the Working Trial and eligibility for Stakes is as for Open Working Trials.

Judges at Championship Working Trials

For C.D. Stake:	Must have judged at least two Open Working Trials and have as a handler qualified a dog 'Excellent' in a Championship C.D. Stake.
For U.D. Stake:	Must have judged U.D. or W.D. Stakes at two Open Trials, have judged C.D. Stake at a Championship Trial and have as a handler qualified a dog 'Excellent' in a Championship W.D. Stake.
For W.D. Stake:	Must have judged U.D. or W.D. Stakes at two Open Trials, U.D. Stake at a Championship Trial and have as a handler qualified a dog 'Excellent' in a Championship W.D. Stake.
For P.D. Stake and T.D. Stake:	Must have judged at two Open Trials. W.D. Stake at a Championship Trial and qualified a dog 'Excellent' in the Stake for which he was nominated to judge. There must be an interval of not less than six calendar months between appointments of the same judge for Championship T.D. and/or P.D. Stakes.
Note:	Service and Police judges are eligible to judge U.D. Stake at a Championship Trial provided they have qualified a dog W.D. 'Excellent'. They must qualify for approval for other Stakes as above, except that those who have judged all parts at Regional or National Police Dog Trials will not have to qualify as a civilian handler.

Kennel Club Working Trial Championships
(a)   The Kennel Club Working Trial Championship at which Police Dog (P.D.) and Tracking Dog (T.D.) Stakes shall be scheduled are held annually.

(b)   The responsibility for organising the Championships each year will normally be delegated to a Working Trial Society approved to hold Championship Working Trials, such Society to be selected by the Working Trials and Obedience Committee from applications submitted by Societies. No Society to stage the event two years in succession.

(c)   The Secretary of the Kennel Club will unless otherwise specified be the Working Trial Secretary for the event, the Society scheduling the Championships appointing a Trials Manager.

(d)   The following shall be the method of selection of judges for the Championships:— Nominated by Working Trials Societies which have been granted Championship Working Trial status for ballotting by Working Trial Council, final selection by the Working Trials and Obedience Committee.

(e)   Dogs eligible for entry in the Championship qualify as follows:—

    (i)   T.D. Championship: A dog must be placed 1st in Championship T.D. Stake and qualified 'Excellent' in the Stake during the period 1st October—30th September preceding the Championships.

    (ii)   P.D. Championship: A dog must have been placed 1st in Championship P.D. Stake and qualified 'Excellent' in the Stake during the period 1st October—30th September in the two years preceding the Championships.

    (iii)   Dogs which qualify as above in both P.D. and T.D. Championship Stakes are permitted to be entered in either or both Championship Stakes.

    (iv)   The Winners of the previous year's Championship Stakes qualify automatically.

    (v)   No other dogs are eligible for entry in the Championships except by special permission of the General Committee of the Kennel Club.

(f)   The Championships will normally be held during the third weekend in October each year.

(g)   The winner of each Stake in the Championships is entitled to the description of Working Trial Champion provided it qualifies 'Excellent'.

(h)   The Working Trial Society selected to hold the Championships is allowed to forego one Open Working Trial during the same year.

Schedule of Exercises and Points
Companion Dog (C.D.) Stake

	Marks	Group Total	Minimum Group Qualifying Mark
Group I.			
1. Heel on Leash	5		
2. Heel Free	10		
3. Recall to Handler	5		
4. Sending the dog away	10	30	21
Group II. Stays			
5. Sit (2 Minutes)	10		
6. Down (10 Minutes)	10	20	14
Group III. Agility			
7. Scale (3) Stay (2) Recall (5)	10		
8. Clear Jump	5		
9. Long Jump	5	20	14
Group IV. Retrieving and Nosework			
10. Retrieve a dumb-bell	10		
11. Elementary Search	20	30	21
Totals	100	100	70

Utility Dog (U.D.) Stake

	Marks	Group Total	Minimum Group Qualifying Mark
Group I. Control			
1. Heel Free	5		
2. Sending the dog away	10		
3. Retrieve a dumb-bell	5		
4. Down (10 Minutes)	10		
5. Steadiness to gunshot	5	35	25
Group II. Agility			
6. Scale (3) Stay (2) Recall (5)	10		
7. Clear Jump	5		
8. Long Jump	5	20	14
Group III. Nosework			
9. Search	35		
10. Track (95) Article (15)	110	145	102
Totals	200	200	141

Working Dog (W.D.) Stake

	Marks	Group Total	Minimum Group Qualifying Mark
Group I. Control			
1. Heel Free	5		
2. Sending the dog away	10		
3. Retrieve a dumb-bell	5		
4. Down (10 Minutes)	10		
5. Steadiness to Gunshot	5	35	25
Group II. Agility			
6. Scale (3) Stay (2) Recall (5)	10		
7. Clear Jump	5		
8. Long Jump	5	20	14
Group III. Nosework			
9. Search	35		
10. Track (90) Articles (10 + 10 = 20)	110	145	102
Totals	200	200	141

Tracking Dog (T.D.) Stake

	Marks	Group Total	Minimum Group Qualifying Mark
Group I. Control			
1. Heel Free	5		
2. Sendaway and Directional Control	10		
3. Speak on Command	5		
4. Down (10 Minutes)	10		
5. Steadiness to Gunshot	5	35	25
Group II. Agility			
6. Scale (3) Stay (2) Recall (5)	10		
7. Clear Jump	5		
8. Long Jump	5	20	14
Group III. Nosework			
9. Search	35		
10. Track (100) Articles (10 + 10 + 10 = 30)	130	165	116
Totals	220	220	155

Police Dog (P.D.) Stake

	Marks	Group Total	Minimum Group Qualifying Mark
Group I. Control			
1. Heel Free	5		
2. Sendaway and Directional Control	10		
3. Speak on Command	5		
4. Down (10 Minutes)	10		
5. Steadiness to Gunshot	5	35	25
Group II. Agility			
6. Scale (3) Stay (2) Recall (5)	10		
7. Clear Jump	5		
8. Long Jump	5	20	14
Group III. Nosework			
9. Search	35		
10. Track (60) Articles (10 + 10 = 20)	80	115	80
Group IV. Patrol			
11. Quartering the Ground	45		
12. Test of Courage	20		
13. Search and Escort	25		
14a. Recall from Criminal	30		
14b. Pursuit and Detention of Criminal	30	150	105
Totals	320	320	224

Description of Exercises and Guidance for Judges and Competitors at Working Trials

A.   Method of Handling — Although implicit obedience to all orders is necessary, dogs and handlers must operate in as free and natural a manner as possible. Excessive formalism may be penalised, particularly if, in the opinion of the Judge, it detracts from the ability of the dog to exercise its senses in relation to all that is happening in the vicinity. Persistent barking, whining etc. in any exercise other than location of articles, person or speak on command should be penalised. Food may not be given to the dog by the handler whilst being tested.

B.   Heel Work — The Judge should test the ability of the dog to keep his shoulder reasonably close to the left knee of the handler who should walk smartly in his natural manner at normal, fast and slow paces through turns and among and around persons and obstacles. The halt, with the dog sitting to heel and a 'figure of eight' may be included at any stage.

Any act, signal or command or jerking of the leash which in the opinion of the Judge has given the dog unfair assistance shall be penalised.

C.   Sit (2 Minutes) — Dogs may be tested individually or in a group or groups. The Judge or Steward will give the command 'last command' and handlers should then instantly give their final commands to the dogs. Any further commands or signals to the dogs will be penalised. Handlers will then be instructed to leave their dogs and proceed to positions indicated by the Judge or Steward until ordered to return to them. Where possible, such positions should be out of sight of the dogs but bearing in mind the short duration of the exercise this may not be practical. Dogs must remain in the sit position throughout the test until the Judge or Steward indicates that the test has finished. Minor movements must be penalised. The Judge may use his discretion should interference by another dog cause the dog to move.

D.   Down (10 Minutes) — Handlers must be out of sight of the dogs who may be tested individually or in a group or groups. The Judge or Steward will give the command 'last command' and handlers should then instantly give their final commands to their dogs. Any further commands or signals to the dogs will be penalised. Handlers will then be instructed to leave their dogs and proceed to positions indicated by the Judge or Steward until ordered to return to them. Dogs must remain in the 'Down' position throughout the test until the Judge or Steward indicates that the Test has finished. No dog will be awarded any marks that sits, stands or crawls more than its approximate body length in any direction. Minor movements must be penalised. The Judge may use his discretion should interference by another dog cause a dog to move. The Judge may test the dogs by using distractions but may not call it by name.

E.   Recall to Handler — The dog should be recalled from the "Down" or "Sit" position. The handler being a reasonable distance from the dog at the discretion of the Judge. The dog should return at a smart pace and sit in front of the handler, afterwards going smartly to heel on command or signal. Handler to await command of the Judge or Steward.

F.   Retrieve a Dumb-Bell — The dog should not move forward to retrieve nor deliver to hand on return until ordered by the handler on the Judge or Stewards' instructions. The Retrieve should be executed at a smart pace without mouthing or playing with the object. After delivery the handler will send his dog to heel on the instructions of the Judge or Steward.

G.   Send Away and Directional Control — The minimum distance that the Judge shall set for the Send Away shall be 20 yards for the C.D. Stake and 50 yards for all other Stakes. The T.D. and P.D. Stakes shall also include a redirection of a minimum of 50 yards. When the dog has reached the designated point or the Judge is satisfied that after a reasonable time the handler cannot improve the position of the dog by any further commands the dog should be stopped in either the stand, sit or down position at the discretion of the handler. At this point in the T.D. or P.D. Stakes the Judge or Steward shall instruct the handler to redirect his dog. In all Stakes, whilst the Judge should take into account the number of commands used during the exercise, importance should be placed upon the handler's ability to direct his dog to the place indicated.

H.   Steadiness to Gunshot – The most appropriate occasion of testing this exercise would be in open country. The dog may be either walking at heel free or be away from the handler who must be permitted to remain within controlling distance whilst the gun is fired. Any sign of fear, aggressiveness or barking must be penalised. This test shall not be carried out without prior warning, or incorporated in any other test. The Judge will not provoke excitement by excessive display of the gun, nor shall the gun be pointed at the dog.

I.   Speak on Command – The Judge will control the position of the handler in relation to the dog and may require the handler to work the dog walking at heel. If the dog is not required to walk at heel, the handler may at his discretion place the dog in the stand, sit or down. The dog will be ordered to speak and cease speaking on command of the Judge or Steward who may then instruct the handler to make the dog speak again. Speaking should be sustained by the dog whilst required with the minimum of commands and/or signals. Continuous and/or excessive incitements to speak shall be severely penalised. This test should not be incorporated with any other test.

J.   Agility – No part of the scale or clear or long jump equipment to be traversed by a dog shall be less than three feet wide nor be in any way injurious to the dog. The tests shall be followed in a sequence agreed by the Judge and will commence with the Scale. The Scale should be a vertical wall of wooden planks and may have affixed on both sides three slats evenly distributed in the top half of the jump. The top surface of the Scale may be lightly padded. The handler should approach the Scale at a walking pace and halt four to nine feet in front of it and in his own time order the dog to scale. On reaching the other side the dog should be ordered to stay in the stand, sit or down position, the handler having previously nominated such a position to the Judge. The Judge should ensure that the dog will stay steady and may indicate to the handler where he should stand in relation to his dog and the Scale before ordering the dog to be recalled over the Scale. A dog which fails to go over the Scale at the second attempt shall be excluded from the stay and recall over the Scale. Failure in the recall over the Scale does not disqualify from marks previously gained.

The handler may either approach the clear and long jumps with the dog or send it forward or stand by the jumps and call the dog up to jump. At no time should the handler proceed beyond any part of the jumps before they have been traversed by the dog. Once the dog has cleared the obstacle he should remain on the other side under control until joined by the handler. The clear jump should be so constructed that it will be obvious if the dog has exerted more than slight pressure upon it. The rigid top bar may be fixed or rest in cups and the space below may be filled in but the filling should not project above the bottom of the top bar. Appreciable pressure exerted by the dog on the clear jump shall be considered to be a failure. Casual fouling with fore or hind legs will be penalised at the discretion of the Judge. Failure or refusal at any of the three types of jump may be followed by a second attempt and any one such failure shall be penalised by at least 50% of the marks allotted to that part of the exercise in which the dog is given a second attempt.

Jumping heights and lengths:

Companion Dog (C.D.) Stake and Utility Dog (U.D.) Stake

(a)   Scale

Dogs not exceeding 10 in. at shoulder	3 ft.
Dogs not exceeding 15 in. at shoulder	4 ft.
Dogs exceeding 15 in. at shoulder	6 ft.

(b)   Clear Jump

Dogs not exceeding 10 in. at shoulder	1 ft. 6 in.
Dogs not exceeding 15 in. at shoulder	2 ft.
Dogs exceeding 15 in. at shoulder	3 ft.

(c)   Long Jump

Dogs not exceeding 10 in. at shoulder	4 ft.
Dogs not exceeding 15 in. at shoulder	6 ft.
Dogs exceeding 15 in. at shoulder	9 ft.

Working Dog (W.D.) Stake, Tracking Dog (T.D.) Stake and Police Dog (P.D.) Stake

(a)	Scale	6 ft.
(b)	Clear Jump	3 ft.
(c)	Long Jump	9 ft.

K. Search — The Companion Dog (C.D.) Stake Search shall contain three articles and all other Stakes shall contain four articles. In all Stakes fresh articles must be placed for each dog who must recover a minimum of two articles to qualify. As a guide the articles should be similar in size to a six inch nail or a match box, but the Judge should choose articles in relation to the nature of the ground and the Stake which he is judging. The time allotted shall be four minutes in the C.D. Stake and five minutes in all other Stakes. The articles should be well handled and placed by a Steward who shall foil the ground by walking in varying directions over the area. Each competitor shall have a separate piece of land.

The C.D. Stake search area shall be 15 yards square, all other Stakes being 25 yards square and shall be clearly defined by a marker peg at each corner. The handler may work his dog from any position outside the area, provided that he does not enter it.

In the C.D. Stake a maximum five marks should be allotted for each article and a maximum five marks for style and control. In all other

Stakes a maximum seven marks should be allotted for each article and a maximum seven marks for style and control.

L.   Track — The track should be plotted on the ground to be used for the nosework by Stewards previous to the day of commencement of the Trials. An area of ground which has had a track laid over it must not have another track laid over it until the following day. The track shall be single line and may include turns. The articles should be in keeping with the nature of the ground. There shall be a marker left by the track layer to indicate the start of the track. In the U.D. Stake a second marker should be left not more than 30 yards from the start to indicate the direction of the first leg.

Unless the Judge considers the dog to have lost the track beyond recovery or has run out of the time allotted for the completion of the track a handler may recast his dog at his discretion. The Judge should not at any time indicate to the handler where he should recast his dog except in exceptional circumstances.

The track shall be approximately half a mile long and should be laid as far as possible by a stranger to the dog. The article(s) should be well scented. When the judging is in progress the track layer should be present at the side of the Judge to indicate the exact line of the track and the position of the articles.

The U.D. Stake track shall not be less than half an hour old and shall include one article at the end, recovery of the article not being a requirement for qualification.

The W.D. and P.D. Stake tracks shall be not less than one and a half hours old and shall include two articles one of which must be recovered to qualify.

The T.D. Stake track shall be not less than three hours old and shall include three articles two of which must be recovered to qualify.

In all Stakes the last article shall indicate the end of the track. No two articles should be laid together.

A spare track additional to requirements should be laid but the opportunity to run a new track should be given only in exceptional circumstances.

The area used for Tracking is out of bounds to all competitors for practice Tracks and exercise from the time of the first track and any competitor found contravening this instruction is liable to be disqualified by the Judge and/or Stewards from participating in the Trial in accordance with the provision of Regulation No. 7(c).

The dog must be worked on a harness and tracking line.

M.   Quartering the Ground — The missing person or criminal should be protected to the minimum extent consistent with safety. He should remain motionless out of sight of the handler, but should be accessible on investigation to a dog which has winded him.

The Judge should satisfy himself that the dog has found the person and has given warning spontaneously and emphatically without being directed by the handler. Once the person has been detected and the dog has given voice, he may offer meat or other food which should be refused by the dog. If the dog ignores the food he may throw it on the ground in front of the dog. A dog which bites the person or criminal must be severely penalised.

N. Test of Courage — This is a test of courage rather than of control. Dogs will not be heavily penalised in this test for lack of control. Handlers must be prepared to have the dog tested when on the lead by an unprotected Judge or Steward, and/or when off the lead by a protected Steward. The method of testing will be at the discretion of the Judge.

O. Search and Escort — The criminal will be searched by the handler with the dog off the lead at the sit, stand or down. The Judge will assess whether the dog is well placed tactically and ready to defend if called to do so.

The handler will then be told to escort the prisoner(s) at least 30 yards in a certain direction, he will give at least one turn on the direction of the Judge. During the exercise the criminal will turn and attempt to overcome the handler. The dog may defend spontaneously or on command and must release the criminal at once both when he stands still or when the handler calls him off. The handler should be questioned as to his tactics in positioning the dog in both search and escort.

P. Recall from Criminal (Exercise 14(a)) — The criminal, protected to the minimim extent consistent with safety, will be introduced to the handler whose dog will be free at heel. After an unheated conversation the criminal will run away. At a reasonable distance the handler will be ordered to send his dog. When the dog is approximately halfway between handler and the criminal he will be ordered to be recalled. The recall may be by whistle or voice. The criminal should continue running until the dog returns or closes. If the dog continues to run alongside the criminal the criminal should run a further ten or dozen paces to indicate this.

Q. Pursuit and Detention of Criminal (Exercise 14(b)) — The criminal (a different one for choice) and handler should be introduced as above, and the dog sent forward under the same conditions. The criminal must continue to attempt to escape and, if possible, should do so through some exit or in some vehicle once the dog has had a chance to catch up with him. The dog must be regarded as having succeeded if it clearly prevents the criminal from continuing his line of flight, either by holding him by the arm, knocking him over or close circling him till he becomes giddy. If the dog fails to make a convincing attempt to detain the criminal, it shall lose any marks that it may have obtained under exercise 14(a) or alternatively, it shall not be tested on exercise 14(a) if that follows exercise 14(b).

Kennel Club Regulations for Tests for Obedience Classes (S2)
1st May, 1976
(Reproduced by kind permission of the Kennel Club)

1. Kennel Club Show Regulations shall where applicable and as amended or varied from time to time apply to Obedience Classes as follows:—

Kennel Club Championship } to Championship Obedience Shows.
Show Regulations.

Kennel Club Licence Show } to Licence Obedience Shows.
Regulations.

Kennel Club Regulations for } to Sanction Obedience Shows.
Sanction Shows.

2. A Show Society may schedule any or all of the following classes at a show. No variation to any test within a class may be made. "Run-offs" will be judged, one at a time, by normal scheduled tests.

Classes may be placed in any order in the schedule but this order must be followed at the show except that a Society, by publication in the schedule, may reserve the right to vary the order of judging when the entry is known.

The maximum number of entries permitted in a Class for one Judge to judge with the exception of Class C where Obedience Certificates are on offer shall be sixty. If this number is exceeded the Class shall be divided by a draw into two equal halves, each to be judged separately. The prizes for each class shall be the same as that offered for the original Class. No Judge shall judge more than sixty dogs in one day and if a Judge is appointed for two or more Classes the combined total entries of which exceed sixty, a Reserve Judge shall be called upon to officiate appropriately. Show Societies should ensure that when appointing Judges for Shows sufficient numbers are appointed for the expected entries. The Reserve Judge may enter dogs for competition at the Show and if not called upon to judge may compete.

Where a Class is divided into two halves exhibitors who have entered for the Class shall be notified accordingly of all changes or alterations and no timed stay exercises are to be held earlier than those advertised for the original class.

In Class C where Obedience Certificates are on offer one Judge only may be appointed for each sex. Should the entries exceed sixty the Judges may approve a Steward who should preferably be a currently active Judge previously approved to judge at a Championship Show, not necessarily for Class C, and who is not a competitor at the show, to report to him the behaviour of the dogs in Sits and Downs in order that the judge might assess the performance. In all classes other than Championship Class C, the same procedure may be adopted should it be expedient to the organising Society. In such cases the steward may be an exhibitor at the show, but not a competitor in the class he is stewarding.

    3. *(a)*   In all the classes the handler may use the dog's name with a command or signal without penalty. Except in the Stay Tests and Distant Control, all tests shall commence and finish with the dog sitting at the handler's side except in Beginners, Novice and Class A Recall Tests when the dog may be left in either the Sit or Down position at the handler's choice.

    (b)   Food shall not be given to a dog in the ring.

    (c)   In any test in which judge's articles are used, none of them should be injurious to the dog, and they must be capable of being picked up by any breed entered in that test.

    (d)   Spayed bitches and castrated dogs are permitted to compete in Obedience Classes.

    (e)   No bitch in season shall be allowed to compete in Obedience Classes.

    (f)   In all tests the points must be graduated.

    (g)   Handlers may use only a slip chain or smooth collar in the ring.

    (h)   Every handler must wear his ring number prominently displayed when in the ring.

    (i)   The Show Executive shall appoint a Chief Steward, whose name must be announced in the schedule, who shall be responsible for the control of any running order and for the smooth running of each class, and whose decision in such matters shall be final.

    (j)   A draw for the order of running in Class C at a Championship Show must be made prior to the Show and exhibitors and judges must be notified of the order of running before the day of the show. Any published order of running must be strictly adhered to. Except for Championship Class C and at Shows where a draw for the running order for all Classes is made Show Managements must ensure that an adequate number of competitors/dogs are available for judging in the first hour following the scheduled time for commencement of judging of that Class. All competitors must report to the ring scoreboard steward and "book in" within one hour of the scheduled commencement of judging for the Class and those reporting late will be excluded from competition unless they have reported previously to the Chief Steward that they are actually working a dog entered in another Championship Class C or in the Stay Test of any other Class.

    In all Scent Tests, dogs should compete in the same order as for previous tests, but the judge may relax the running order where necessary. Scent tests must not be carried out during the main ring work but will take place as a separate test at the judges' discretion.

(k) Judging rings shall not in any circumstances contain less than 900 square feet of clear floor space and shall not be less than 20 feet in width except that for Championship Class C the ring must contain not less than 1,600 square feet.

(l) No person shall carry out punitive correction or harsh handling of a dog at any time whilst within the boundaries of the show.

(m) Judges at Championship Shows

(1) For Class C at Championship Shows judges must have had at least three years' judging experience and must have judged at twenty Open Obedience Shows at which they must have judged Class C not less than twelve times.

(2) For all other classes, other than Class C, judges must have had at least two years' judging experience and must have judged at eight Open Obedience Shows.

(n) A judge of Class C at an Open Show must record in the judging book the number of points awarded to each dog with 290 or more points. The Show Secretary will record these in the official marked catalogue.

4. Imperfections in heeling between tests will not be judged but any physical disciplining by the handler in the ring, or any uncontrolled behaviour of the dog, such as snapping, unjustified barking, fouling the ring, or running out of the ring, even between tests, must be penalised by deducting points from the total score and the judge may bar the dog from further competition in that class.

5. *(a)* In all the following Definitions of Classes, First Prize wins in Limited and Sanction Show Obedience Classes will not count for entry in Open and Championship Show Obedience Classes. No dog is eligible to compete in Obedience Classes at Limited and Sanction Shows which has won an Obedience Certificate or obtained any award that counts towards the title of Obedience Champion or the equivalent thereof under the rules of any governing body recognised by the Kennel Club. Obedience Champions are eligible only for Class C at Open and Championship Shows.

(b) A dog must be entered in the lowest class for which it is eligible by definition and may also be entered in the next highest class if desired, with the exception of Championship Class C for which dogs appropriately qualified only may be entered.

BEGINNERS — If owner or handler or dog have won a total of two or more first prizes in the Beginners Class, they may not compete in Beginners. Winners of one first prize in any other Obedience Class are ineligible to compete in this Class.

Handlers will not be penalised for encouragement or extra commands except in the Sit and Down tests. In these tests, at the discretion of the judge, handlers may face their dogs. Judges or stewards must not use the words 'last command' except in the Sit and Down tests.

1. Heel on Lead   15 points
2. Heel Free   20 points
3. Recall from sit or down position at handler's choice.
   Dog to be recalled by handler, when stationary and
   facing the dog. Dog to return smartly to handler, sit
   in front, go to heel — all on command of judge or
   steward to handler. Distance at discretion of judge.
   Test commences when handler leaves dog   10 points
4. Retrieve any article. Handlers may use their own article   25 points
5. Sit One Minute, handler in sight   10 points
6. Down Two Minutes, handler in sight   20 points
                                             Total   100 points

NOVICE — For dogs that have not won two first prizes in Obedience
Classes (Beginners Classes excepted).
    Handlers will not be penalised for encouragement or extra commands
except in the Sit and Down tests. In these tests, at the discretion of the
judge, handlers may face their dogs. Judges or stewards must not use
the words 'last command' except in the Sit and Down tests.
1. Temperament Test. To take place immediately before
   heel on lead. Dog to be on lead in the Stand position.
   Handler to stand by dog. Judge to approach quietly
   from the front and to run his hand gently down the
   dog's back. Judge may talk quietly to dog to reassure
   it. Any undue resentment, cringing, growling or
   snapping to be penalised. This is not a stand for
   examination or stay test   10 points
2. Heel on Lead   10 points
3. Heel Free   20 points
4. Recall from sit or down position at handler's choice.
   Dog to be recalled by handler when stationary and
   facing the dog. Dog to return smartly to handler, sit
   in front, go to heel — all on command of judge or
   steward to handler. Distance at discretion of judge.
   Test commences when handler leaves dog   10 points
5. Retrieve a Dumb-bell. Handlers may use their own
   bells   20 points
6. Sit One Minute, handler in sight   10 points
7. Down Two Minutes, handler in sight   20 points
                                             Total   100 points

CLASS A — For dogs which have not won four first prizes in Classes A
and B in total.
    Simultaneous command and signal will be permitted. Extra com-
mands or signals must be penalised.
1. Heel on Lead   15 points
2. Temperament Test. Will take place before Heel Free.
   Dog to be in the stand position and off lead. Handler

to stand beside dog. Conditions as for Novice Temperament Test, except that Test will commence with order 'last command' and end with order 'test finished'. Extra commands will be penalised. This is not a stand for examination or stay test   10 points
3. Heel Free   20 points
4. Recall from Sit or Down, position at handler's choice. Dog to be recalled to heel by handler, on command of judge or steward, whilst handler is walking away from dog, both to continue forward until halted. The recall and halt points to be the same for each dog and handler. Test commences following handler's last command to dog   15 points
5. Retrieve a Dumb-bell. Handlers may use their own dumb-bells   20 points
6. Sit One Minute, handler in sight   10 points
7. Down Five Minutes, handler out of sight   30 points
8. Scent Discrimination, handler's scent on handler's article. The total number of articles shall not exceed ten, all of which shall be clearly visible to the dog   30 points

                                               Total   150 points

CLASS B — For dogs which have not won four first prizes in Class B and Open Class C in total.

One command, by word or signal, except in Test 2. Extra commands or signals must be penalised.
1. Heel Free. The dog shall be required to walk at heel free and shall also be tested at fast and slow pace. Each change of pace shall commence from the 'halt' position   30 points
2. Send Away, Drop and Recall. On command of judge to handler, dog to be sent away in direction indicated by judge. After the dog has been dropped, handler will call the dog to heel whilst walking where directed by judge and both will continue forward. No obstacle to be placed in path of dog. Simultaneous command and signal is permitted but as soon as the dog leaves the handler the arm must be dropped. (N.B. an extra command may be simultaneous command and signal, but an extra command must be penalised   40 points
3. Retrieve any one article provided by the Judge but which must not be in any manner injurious to the dog (definitely excluding food or glass). The article to be picked up easily by any breed of dog in that Class and to be clearly visible to the dog. A separate similar article to be used for each dog. Test commences following Judge or Steward's words 'last command' to handler   30 points

4. Stand One Minute, handler at least ten paces away
   from and facing away from the dog   10 points
5. Sit Two Minutes, handler out of sight   20 points
6. Down Ten Minutes, handler out of sight   40 points
7. Scent Discrimination. Handler's scent on article pro-
   vided by judge. A separate similar article to be used
   for each dog and the total number of articles shall not
   exceed ten, all of which shall be clearly visible to the
   dog and shall be similar to the article given to the
   handler. Judges must use a separate similar scent
   decoy or decoys for each dog. No points will be
   awarded if the article is given to the dog   30 points

                                                           Total   200 points

CLASS C— At Championship Shows: For dogs which have won four first
prizes in Class B, or Open Class C have gained 290 marks on no less
than three occasions under three different Judges in Open Class C and
have been placed not lower than third on one occasion in Open Class C.
Dogs which qualified for entry in Championship Class C prior to 1st
May 1976 are also eligible.

At Open Shows: For dogs which have won four first prizes in Classes
A or B in total.

At Limited and Sanction Shows: Open to all dogs except Obedience
Certificate winners and dogs which have obtained any award that counts
towards the title of Obedience Champion or the equivalent thereof
under the rules of any governing body recognised by the Kennel Club.

One command, by word or signal, except in Test 2 where an extra
command may be simultaneous command and signal. Extra commands
or signals must be penalised.

1. Heel Work. The dog shall be required to walk at heel
   free, and also be tested at fast and slow pace. At some
   time during this test, at the discretion of the Judge,
   the dog shall be required, whilst walking at heel at
   normal pace, to be left at the Stand, Sit and Down in
   any order (the order to be the same for each dog) as
   and when directed by the judge. The handler shall
   continue forward alone, without hesitation, and continue as directed by the Judge until he reaches his dog
   when both shall continue forward together until
   halted. Heel work may include left about turns and
   figure-of-eight at normal and/or slow pace   60 points
2. Send Away, Drop and Recall as in Class B   40 points
3. Retrieve any one article provided by the Judge but
   which must not be in any manner injurious to the dog
   (definitely excluding food or glass). The article to be
   picked up easily by any breed of dog in that Class and
   to be clearly visible to the dog. A separate article to

be used for each dog. Test commences following
Judge or Steward's 'last command' to handler   30 points
4. Distant Control. Dog to Sit, Stand and Down at a
marked place not less than ten paces from handler, in
any order on command from judge to handler. Six
instructions to be given in the same order for each
dog. Excessive movement, i.e. more than the length
of the dog, in any direction by the dog, having
regard to its size, will be penalised. The dog shall start
the exercise with its front feet behind a designated
point. No penalty for excessive movement in a forward
direction shall be imposed until the back legs of the
dog pass the designated point   50 points
5. Sit Two Minutes, handler out of sight   20 points
6. Down Ten Minutes, handler out of sight   50 points
7. Scent Discrimination. Judge's scent on piece of
marked cloth. Neutral and decoy cloths to be provided
by the Show Executive. The judge shall not place his
cloth in the ring himself, but it shall be placed by a
steward. A separate similar piece to be used for each
dog and the total number of separate similar pieces of
cloth from which the dog shall discriminate shall not
exceed ten. If a dog fetches or fouls a wrong article
this must be replaced by a fresh article. At open-air
shows all scent cloths must be adequately weighted
to prevent them being blown about. The method of
taking scent shall be at the handler's discretion but
shall not require the judge to place his hand on or
lean towards the dog. A separate similar piece of
cloth approximately 6 in. by 6 in. but not more than
10 in. by 10 in. shall be available to be used for giving
each dog the scent. Judges should use a scent decoy
or decoys   50 points
                                              Total   300 points

6.   The Kennel Club will offer an Obedience Certificate (Dog) and
an Obedience Certificate (Bitch) for winners of 1st prizes in Class C
Dog and Class C Bitch at a Championship Show, provided that the
exhibits do not lose more than 10 points out of 300, and provided also
that the classes are open to all breeds.

Judges must also award a Reserve Best of Sex provided that the
exhibit has not lost more than 10 points out of 300.

7.   The Kennel Club will offer at Crufts Dog Show each year the
Kennel Club Obedience Championship—(Dog) and the Kennel Club
Obedience Championship—(Bitch). A dog awarded one or more
Obedience Certificates during the calendar year preceding Crufts Show
shall be entitled to compete.

The Tests for the Championships shall be those required for Class C in these Regulations. If the winning dog or bitch has lost more than 10 points out of 300, the Championship award shall be withheld.

8.   As provided in Kennel Club Rule 4(c), the following dogs shall be entitled to be described as Obedience Champions and shall receive a Certificate to that extent from the Kennel Club: —

(a)   The winners of the Kennel Club Obedience Championships.

(b)   A dog awarded three Obedience Certificates under three different judges in accordance with these Regulations.

EXPLANATORY NOTES FOR OBEDIENCE TESTS
(To be read in conjunction with regulations S(2)

In all classes the dog should work in a happy manner and prime consideration should be given to judging the dog and handler as a team. The dog may be encouraged and praised except where specifically stated.

Instructions and commands to competitors may be made either by the judge or his steward by delegation..

In all tests the left side of a handler will be regarded as the 'working side', unless the handler suffers from a physical disability and has the judge's permission to work the dog on the right-hand side.

To signal the completion of each test the handler will be given the command 'test finished'.

It is permissible for handlers to practise their dogs before going into the ring provided there is no punitive correction and this is similar to an athlete limbering up before an event.

Timetable of Judging — To assist show executives the following guide timetable is issued: —

Class C	6 dogs per hour
Class B	8 dogs per hour
Class A	12 dogs per hour
Novice.	12 dogs per hour
Beginners.	12 dogs per hour

The dog should be led into the ring for judging with a collar and lead attached (unless otherwise directed) and should be at the handler's side.

1. Heel on Lead — The dog should be sitting straight at the handler's side. On command the handler should walk briskly forward in a straight line with the dog at heel. The dog should be approximately level with and reasonably close to the handler's leg at all times when the handler is walking. The lead must be slack at all times. On the command 'Left Turn' or 'Right Turn' the handler should return smartly at a right angle in the appropriate direction and the dog should keep its position at the handler's side. Unless otherwise directed, at the command 'about turn' the handler should turn about smartly on the spot through an angle of 180° to the right and walk in the opposite direction, the dog maintaining its position at the handler's side. On the command 'halt' the handler should halt immediately and the dog should sit straight at the handler's

side. Throughout this test the handler may not touch the dog or make use of the lead without penalty.

2. Heel Free — This test should be carried out in a similar manner as for Heel on Lead except that the dog must be off the lead throughout the test.

3. Retrieve a Dumb-Bell/Article — At the start of this exercise the dog should be sitting at the handler's side. On command the handler must throw the dumb-bell/article in the direction indicated. The dog should remain at the Sit position until the handler is ordered to send it to retrieve the dumb-bell/article. The dog should move out promptly at a smart pace to collect the dumb-bell/article cleanly. It should return with the dumb-bell/article at a smart pace and sit straight in front of the handler. On command the handler should take the dumb-bell/article from the dog. On further command the dog should be sent to heel. In Classes A, B and C the test commences on the order 'last command' to handler.

4. (a)   Sit/Stay — The Judge or Steward will direct handlers to positions in the ring. The command 'last command' will be given when all are ready and handlers should then instantly give their final command to the dogs. Any further commands or signals to the dogs after this 'last command' will be penalised. Handlers will then be instructed to leave their dogs and walk to positions indicated until ordered to return to them. Dogs should remain at the Sit position throughout the test. This is a group test and all dogs must compete together.

(b)   Stand/Stay — This test should be carried out exactly as for the Sit/Stay, except that dogs will be left in the Stand position throughout the Test. This is a group test and all dogs must compete together.

(c)   Down/Stay — This test should be carried out exactly as for the Sit/Stay, except that dogs will be left in the Down position throughout the Test. This is a group test and all dogs must compete together.

5. Scent Discrimination — A steward will place the scented article amongst up to a maximum of nine other articles.

In a scent test if a dog brings in a wrong article or physically fouls any article (i.e. mouths it) this article will be replaced.

The dog should at this time be facing away from the articles. On command the handler should bring the dog to a point indicated, give the dog scent and stand upright before sending the dog to find and retrieve the appropriate article. The dog should find the article and complete the test as for the Retrieve test. In all tests, scent articles are to be placed at least 2 feet apart. Limiting the time allowed for this test is at the Judge's discretion.

Class A — Handler's Scent on Handler's Article.

The Judge should reject any articles he considers to be unfit by nature of their size, shape or substance and which in his opinion could have the effect of converting this elementary Scent Test into a Sight Test. In this test at least one other article must be scented by someone other than the handler and the decoy article(s) must be similar for each dog.

Class B — Handler's Scent on Article provided by the Judge.
The article must not be given to the dog. All articles must be separate and similar.

Class C — Judge's Scent on piece of marked cloth. A decoy steward should not handle a cloth for a period longer than the Judge.

Extract from American Kennel Club Obedience Regulations for Utility Class Scent Discrimination
(Reproduced by kind permission of the American Kennel Club)

The principal features of these exercises are the selection of the handler's article from among the other articles by scent alone, and the prompt delivery of the right article to the handler.

Orders are 'Send your dog', 'Take it' and 'Finish'.

In each of these two exericises the dog must select by scent alone and retrieve an article which has been handled by its handler. The articles shall be provided by the handler and shall consist of two sets, each comprised of five identical objects not more than six inches in length, which may be items of everyday use. One set shall be made entirely of rigid metal, and one of leather of such design that nothing but leather is visible except for the minimum amount of thread or metal necessary to hold the object together. The articles in each set must be legibly numbered, each with a different number and must be approved by the judge.

The handler shall present all ten articles to the judge, who shall designate one from each set and make written note of the numbers of the two articles he has selected. These two handler's articles shall be placed on a table or chair within the ring until picked up by the handler, who shall hold in his hand only one article at a time. The judge or steward will handle each of the remaining eight articles as he places them on the floor or ground about fifteen feet in front of the handler and dog, at random about six inches apart. The judge must make sure that the articles are properly separated before the dog is sent, so that there may be no confusion of scent between the articles.

Handler and dog shall turn around after watching the judge or steward spread the articles, and shall remain facing away from those articles until the judge has taken the handler's scented article and given the order, 'Send your dog'.

The handler may use either article first, but must relinquish each one immediately when ordered by the judge. The judge shall make certain that the handler imparts his scent to each article only with his hands and that, between the time the handler picks up each article and the time he gives it to the judge, the article is held continuously in the handler's hands which must remain in plain sight.

On order from the judge, the handler will immediately place his article on the judge's book or work sheet. The judge, without touching the article with his hands, will place it among those on the ground or floor.

On order from the judge to 'Send your dog', the handler may give the command to Heel before turning, and will execute a Right about Turn, stopping to face the articles, the dog in the Heel Position. The handler shall then give the command or signal to retrieve. Handlers may at their discretion on orders from the judge to 'Send your dog', execute with their dog a Right about Turn to face the articles, simultaneously giving the command or signal to retrieve. In this instance the dog shall not assume a sitting position, but shall go directly to the articles. The handler may give his scent to the dog by gently touching the dog's nose with the palm of one open hand, but this may only be done while the dog and handler have their backs to the articles and the arm and hand must be returned to a natural position before handler and dog turn to face the articles.

The dog shall go at a brisk pace to the articles. It may take any reasonable time to select the right article, but only provided it works continuously. After picking up the right article the dog shall return at a brisk pace and complete the exercise as in the Retrieve on the Flat.

These procedures shall be followed for both articles. Should a dog retrieve a wrong article in the first exercise, that article shall be placed on the table or chair. The correct article must be removed, and the second exercise shall be conducted with one less article on the ground or floor.

Scoring
Deductions shall be the same as in the Retrieve on the Flat. In addition, a dog that fails to go out to the group of articles, or retrieves a wrong article, or fails to bring the right article to the handler, must be scored zero for the particular exercise.

Substantial deductions shall be made for a dog that picks up a wrong article, even though he puts it down again immediately, for any roughness by the handler in impairing his scent to the dog, and for any excessive motions by the handler in turning to face the articles.

Minor or substantial deductions, depending on the circumstances in each case, shall be made for a dog that is slow or inattentive, or that does not work continuously. There shall be no penalty for a dog that takes a reasonably long time examining the articles provided the dog works smartly and continuously.

Index

Page numbers in *italics* refer to the illustrations